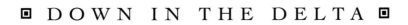

◙ DOWN IN THE DELTA ◙

DOWN IN
THE DELTA

■ A SCREENPLAY ■

MYRON E. GOBLE

Introduction by Maya Angelou

HYPERION

MIRAMAX
BOOKS

NEW YORK

Library of Congress Cataloging-in-Publication Data

Goble, Myron.
    Down in the delta . a screenplay / Myron Goble : introduction by
Maya Angelou — 1st ed.
        p.   cm.
    ISBN 0-7868-8458-4
    I. Down in the delta (Motion picture)   II. Title.
PN1997.D72   1998
791.43'72—dc21   98–42800
                                                              CIP

Book design by Kathy Kikkert

First Edition

10 9 8 7 6 5 4 3 2 1

I would not be experiencing the full rainbow of joys provided by the writing
of this screenplay, if not for the contributions of four generous women:

MARY ELIZABETH GOBLE

Because of those *National Geographics* and *Reader's Digest Condensed Books*,
I still ask *"Why?"* as often as did that sugar-crazed five-year-old.

MAYA ANGELOU

What could bring more pleasure than finally seeing the film that I wrote?
Seeing the film that I *meant* to write.

GEE NICHOLL

The Fellowship sustained me for an important year,
but the encouragement will stay with me forever.

MURIEL DIMEN

Accompanied by loving eyes and a reassuring smile,
I have the chance to do everything right.

With Joy, Faith, Hope, Peace and Love . . .
Myron

◙ FOREWORD ◙

Folktales are told and retold the world over. They have the intimacy of memory and the likeness of family members. They are known so well that they are often taken for granted and their meanings and their worth are frequently discounted. Their staying power, however, can be credited to the fact that they continue to contain human wit and wisdom. The Brer Rabbit tales of the American South, the Ananse tales of West Africa, the Eddas of Scandinavia, the Renard stories of France, as well as the sagas from the shtetels of Russia bear the burden of knowledge learned and relearned over centuries.

Down In the Delta is an original tale written by a highly original writer, Myron Goble, and is a folktale in the classic manner. It could have been told in Paris, France, or Paris, Texas, in Canton, Ohio, or Canton, China, or in any human gathering where the broad values are the same.

Greed, ignorance, tenderness, violence, love, hate and a longing for self-destruction are to be found in Goble's screenplay even as they are found in everyday human life. The characters in *Down In the Delta* are not larger than life, they are the stuff of life, which means that each of them is accessible to each of us. They are sometimes likable, sometimes contrary, amusing or aggravating, but they are always comprehensible.

When the story shows the characters with all their foibles and frailties overcoming adversity, when it reveals that the characters can survive, and in fact even thrive, the listeners, the viewers and readers are lifted up from the base of ennui and cynicism into the rare light of positive possibilities.

Goble's script gave me the opportunity to continue the effort I make in all my work. I do believe that pride resides even in debased submission, and that victory can be wrenched from the ravenous teeth of defeat. Since I am convinced that events are always positive and negative, it was fitting that we shot *Down In the Delta* up in Toronto, and that in the play a rambunctious denison from the Chicago depths could become, before our eyes, a responsible, gracious lady on the southern landscape. That is the real material of folktales the world over.

Maya Angelou

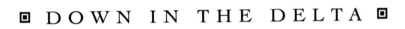

◙ DOWN IN THE DELTA ◙

FADE IN:

TIGHT ON A MEMORABLE ENVELOPE

Filled but not yet sealed; addressed but not yet stamped.

Now the camera reveals that it's propped atop a fireplace mantel, flanked on both sides by knickknacks. When an aged and male African-American HAND enters frame to remove it, we linger on the EMPTY SPACE left behind.

WOOD TABLETOP

Fingers carefully seal the envelope, then turn it over to rub on a stamp. It's addressed to Chicago.

EXT. COUNTRY-STYLE METAL MAILBOX—DAY

The hand places the envelope inside, then raises the red "outgoing mail" signal flag.

Now the camera reveals that the mailbox indeed sits atop a post alongside a gravel country road, surrounded by green fields that melt into the horizon.

EXT. CHICAGO SKYLINE—JUNE MORNING

The towers stand tall and proud against the clear, blue sky.

EXT. CHICAGO HOUSING PROJECT—MORNING

Hulking fortresses of concrete block—graffiti on too many walls, plywood over too many windows.

INT. PROJECT APARTMENT—MORNING

An impersonal shell made cozy home, with many pictures hung and keepsakes displayed. Faded by time, but spotless.

INT. KITCHEN/EATING AREA — MORNING

ROSA LYNN SINCLAIR, an energetic, mid-sixties African American woman, scrubs a frying pan in the sink. Her twelve-year-old grandson THOMAS feeds a hyperactive three-year-old TRACY at the table.

> ROSA LYNN
>
> I want you home by three. Not three thirty, not three fifteen, but three.

> THOMAS
>
> Yes, ma'am.

(Warily extends Pop Tart.)

> C'mon, Tracy . . . Put some in your mouth.

Tracy snatches it and smears it on his head. Thomas slumps, unbuckles the belt that restrains her to the chair, and she runs to a wall and grunts as she fingerpaints with Pop Tart.

Rosa Lynn briskly dries the now-gleaming pan.

> ROSA LYNN
>
> Don't you forget her bottle now.

As Thomas carefully pours milk from his cereal bowl into a baby bottle, Rosa Lynn silently places a large damp sponge on the table beside him and exits. Thomas stares first at the sponge, then at the waiting Pop-Tarted wall.

INT. LIVING ROOM — A LITTLE LATER

On the couch, Rosa Lynn meticulously cuts food coupons from a newspaper. Thomas is perched beside her, wearing a little knapsack. Tracy plays "hot potato" with her bottle on the floor — hurls it down, yanks it up, hurls it down again.

ROSA LYNN

If your Mama isn't home soon, you're gonna have to
stay home and watch Tracy.
(Off his solemn shrug; she caresses his head.)
Maybe you should read a book or something while
you're waiting . . . ?

*We hear locks turn and LORETTA enters. She's late thirties and might be
pretty, but now looks too haggard. Rosa Lynn's demeanor immediately stiffens.*

ROSA LYNN

Loretta, where have you been?

*Loretta heads straight for the bathroom, with Rosa Lynn closing in fast. The
door slams right in Rosa Lynn's face.*

ROSA LYNN

Now how you gonna find a job, when you're out playin'
all night? You tell me that!

*Thomas deposits Tracy and bottle into a modified crib that's more like a covered
cage. Howling, she tries to escape, then grabs a large, stuffed TIGER to either
hug or strangle it.*

ROSA LYNN

C'mon, Thomas.

*She folds the clipped coupons into the overflowing Bible that serves as spiritual
and practical Filofax. As she sets the alarm clock beside it, she calls to the
bathroom door:*

ROSA LYNN

We already wasted enough time this mornin'!

*She picks up her big canvas shopping bag, reaches through the cage's bars to give
Tracy's wailing head a parting caress, then they exit. After the locks turn, the
bathroom door opens a crack and Loretta warily peeks out.*

EXT. BUILDING'S ENTRANCE—DAY

Parked in the circular drive is a new, fire-engine red Jeep Wrangler, top down and music pounding. MARCO, enthroned atop the back of the driver's seat, holds court among his crew.

Rosa Lynn and Thomas pass on the adjacent sidewalk.

> **MARCO**
> *(taunting smile)*
> Hey, Miss Rosa.
> *(She ignores him.)*
> How you doin' today?

Thomas glances at Marco and all his riches.

> **THOMAS**
> Hey, Marco.

> **ROSA LYNN**
> Eyes straight ahead, please.

> **MARCO**
> Yo, Thomas! You 'bout ready to make some real money?
> *(Rosa Lynn stops.)*
> 'Nough money to buy some dope-fresh new sneakers ev'ry day of the week?

> **ROSA LYNN**
> *(to Thomas)*
> You get along to your business.
> *(He hesitates)*
> Go on.
> *(as he walks away.)*
> I want you home by *three*, you hear me?

Rosa Lynn approaches Marco, neither intimidated by the other.

ROSA LYNN
You stay away from my Thomas.

MARCO
(exaggerated deference)
Yes, ma'am, anything you say.
(She turns to leave.)
But is he gonna stay away from me?

Marco smiles at her stiff, departing back.

EXT. CITY BUS STOP—DAY

Waiting for a bus, Thomas alternately listens on the earphones of his memorably bright yellow Walkman, then speaks aloud, apparently repeating along with the tape:

THOMAS
I can do it. . . . *I* can do it. . . .

As he continues, he focuses on the cover of the tape box:
BLACK FINANCIAL POWER: YOU CAN DO IT!

THOMAS
I *can* do it. . . . I *can* do it. . . .

EXT. POOR NEIGHBORHOOD—DAY

Rosa Lynn enters a small church's administrative building.

INT. CHURCH SOUP KITCHEN—DAY

As Rosa Lynn tersely puts on an apron:

OLDER VOLUNTEER
Loretta?
(Rosa Lynn nods.)
The devil is so strong. . . . *So strong!*

EXT. RECREATIONAL PIER—DAY

Establishing shot. Football-field-size, jutting far out into Lake Michigan, its profile dominated by a ferris wheel.

EXT. PIER—CARNIVAL AREA—DAY

Near the ferris wheel, it's quiet and still, except for a few carnival workers opening up stalls and the TOURIST COUPLE who stand at water's edge and gawk at the skyline.

> TOURIST WOMAN
> *(deep southern accent)*
> Will you take a look at that? They really are like broad shoulders.

> TOURIST MAN
> *(antsy, looks at his watch)*
> Uh-huh. C'mon, we gotta check outta the hotel.

> TOURIST WOMAN
> Will you just relax? We've got plenty of time.

NEARBY LOCATION

Observing them from the shadows, Thomas smiles with anticipation, removes his knapsack and slowly pulls out a Polaroid camera.

INT. APARTMENT—DAY

Loretta snores on the couch. Tracy stares and growls as she bangs her near empty bottle against the bars of her cage.

INT. CHURCH SOUP KITCHEN—DAY

Rosa Lynn works a serving line. The approaching HOMELESS MAN eyes her with apprehension. She eyes him skeptically.

ROSA LYNN
I thought you said your wife was takin' you back in. . . .

HOMELESS MAN
She did, for awhile. But . . .
(trails off, shrugs)

Rosa Lynn rolls her eyes, then softens and makes sure he gets a full bowl and an extra piece of bread.

EXT. RECREATIONAL PIER—DAY

TIGHT ON A POLAROID PICTURE of the TOURIST COUPLE posing against the Chicago skyline they were admiring earlier.

Now the camera reveals that the picture is being held by the TOURIST WOMAN.

THOMAS
Five dollars.

TOURIST MAN
She already got a whole suitcase full of souvenir junk
to drag home. . . .

THOMAS
Yo, man . . . how much money you pay to see Chicago?
What's 'nother five dollars to take it home with you?

The TOURIST MAN shrugs, smiles, reaches into his pocket.

INT. APARTMENT—DAY

Alarm clanging, telephone ringing, Tracy wailing and banging—even yelling and pounding coming from the neighbors' side of the wall. Loretta jerks awake on the couch, slaps off the alarm and staggers over to yank the phone from its hook.

LORETTA

Yeah?!

A steady stream erupts from the receiver. Cradling her head:

LORETTA

No, not yet, I haven't had a —
(*turns defensive*)
I was *just* gettin' ready to —

INTERCUT WITH:

INT. CHURCH SOUP KITCHEN — DAY

Rosa Lynn is in her apron and unfazed by the sounds of holy hell breaking loose on the payphone's receiver.

ROSA LYNN

— And when you gonna take your baby daughter outta
that crib and show her some love?! You tell me that! . . .

INT. APARTMENT — DAY

Wailing/banging/pounding/yelling/harping sends Loretta right to the edge:

LORETTA

I *said* I was goin' to, and I *am*, OK?! So just get off my
back!
(*slams down the phone*)

INT. CHURCH SOUP KITCHEN — DAY

Rosa Lynn hangs up with serene satisfaction.

INT. APARTMENT — DAY

Loretta lunges and slams her palm into the pounding wall. The crash of glass on the other side, followed by an anguished yelp. Loretta roars at the wall:

LORETTA

Now you shut the hell up, or I'm comin' on over there!

Abrupt silence on the other side. Loretta nods once, then picks up her bag to fish out a pint bottle which, to her disappointment, is empty. Realizing Tracy's wails:

LORETTA

OK, OK, quiet down. . . . Mama's gonna fix you somethin'. . . .

She goes to the kitchen and returns with a Coke, retrieves Tracy's bottle, pours some in with the remaining milk and passes it back through. Contemplating the nursing toddler:

LORETTA

Can you say Mama?
(coaxes)
C'mon, Tracy . . . say, Ma . . . Ma.

Tracy stares and snuffles and sucks on the muddy mixture.

LATER, SAME LOCATION

Rosa Lynn enters to find Loretta snoring and Tracy wailing. She picks up Tracy, and winces at her soiled diapers. Eyeing Loretta with disappointment that borders on disgust, she carries the wriggling/wailing Tracy toward the bathroom.

ROSA LYNN

C'mon, Tracy. Let's go make you all pretty again. . . .

EXT. PROJECTS — NIGHT

A dark, deadly, no-man's land. The distant sounds of sirens and random gunfire. Closer by, that of glass breaking, followed by the whoop of a car's burglar alarm.

INT. APARTMENT — NIGHT

The gunfire is distant, but still too discernable. On the sofa, with a drooling Tracy asleep on her lap, Rosa Lynn reads a letter and idly strokes Tracy's hair.

ROSA LYNN
(pleased)

Well, listen here. . . . Your Uncle Earl says that Cousin
Rankin's funeral was real nice, folks came from all over
the county for it. . . . Oh, Aunt Annie couldn't go. She
was havin' a bad day.

(looks up)

She's gettin' a little slow, you know.

Loretta and Thomas are playfully crouched beneath the closed drapes of the
window. After a particularly rapid series of gunfire, Thomas quizzically looks at
Loretta.

LORETTA

AK-47?

THOMAS

Not 'nough spit.

(listens to a repeat)

That be a Big Mack.

(off her skepticism)

Pah!-Pah!-Pah!-Pah!-Pah!

Loretta concedes to his expertise.

ROSA LYNN
(still reading)

Well, I'll be! Earl says they just bought themselves a
brand-new car!

(touch of sarcasm)

My, they must be doin' well.

THOMAS

If he so rich, how come he don't send us some money?

Loretta smiles and perfectly lip-syncs:

ROSA LYNN (OS)

Hmph! We don't need nothin' from nobody!

Thomas grins at Loretta's own expertise.

LORETTA

How come he's writin' all of a sudden? I thought you
two didn't get along so good.

ROSA LYNN

He's writing because he wants something from me.

THOMAS

What we got that he want?

*Rosa Lynn folds the letter back into the memorable envelope from the opening
scene, eases Tracy's dead weight to the sofa beside her, then opens the Bible to file
the envelope among other papers already there. Loretta stands and stretches.*

ROSA LYNN
(to Thomas)

Would you like to go up to Raymond's and watch TV
for a while?

THOMAS
(dashes for the door)

Yes, ma'am!

ROSA LYNN

I want you home by ten, you hear me?
(as the door closes)
You stay *off* that elevator, and don't you make me come
up there lookin' for you!
(Loretta edges for the bathroom.)
Loretta, we got to talk.

Loretta sullenly leans against the wall.

ROSA LYNN

You ever think 'bout where we gonna be five years from now?

(off Loretta's silence)

Dead. Me from old age, you from drinkin' or worse, and Thomas shot up in the street.

Loretta sighs and sits down.

LATER, SAME LOCATION

The two women haven't budged from their physical or attitudinal positions.

LORETTA

(frustrated)

You just don't get it, do you? There aren't any jobs out there! I've looked and looked!

ROSA LYNN

There's got to be somethin' . . . I'm telling you, somethin' new happens in this world ev'ry single day. You just gotta keep at it.

Loretta sadly stares across the room.

WHAT SHE SEES: Tracy in her cage, asleep like an angel.

ROSA LYNN

(gently)

She is not your fault.

(Loretta looks at her.)

She is not a fault at all, she's a blessing. And the sooner you realize that, the sooner you'll get on with things.

Loretta leans back and gazes up towards the ceiling.

INT. GROCERY STORE — DAY

Loretta pushes the cart while Thomas references coupons to pull items from the shelves. When she sneaks in something extra, Thomas disapprovingly pulls it from the cart.

> THOMAS
> Gramma Rosa say get what's on her list and *nothin'* else!

Loretta wistfully eyes a jar of styling grease. Thomas hesitates, then silently pulls it down and puts it in the cart.

INT. GROCERY STORE — CHECKOUT LINE — DAY

In line to pay, Thomas sees a small CASHIER WANTED sign.

> THOMAS
> Looka that. . . .

LORETTA
(reads)
I couldn't get that job. You know I can't add and
subtract too good.

Thomas indicates the scanning system and automated register.

THOMAS
Even Tracy can do that. At least ask 'em 'bout it.
(entices her)
It get Gramma Rosa off your back . . .

Loretta shrugs and approaches the elevated manager's booth. Thomas looks
around, then surreptitiously removes the sign.

INT. APARTMENT—NIGHT

Loretta hovers over Thomas as he fills out an application.

LORETTA
How much school you givin' me?

THOMAS
(chortling)
A coupla years junior college . . .

LORETTA
You think that'll be 'nough?

Seated nearby, Rosa Lynn beams her approval.

ROSA LYNN
Don't you worry 'bout a thing! You gonna get that job.
. . . I can *feel* it!

Off Rosa Lynn's enthusiasm, even Loretta looks confident.

INT. APARTMENT—MORNING

Freshly groomed and perhaps overdressed in her Sunday Best, Loretta shyly poses.

>   LORETTA
> You don't think this is too fancy?

>   ROSA LYNN
>   *(nods her approval)*
> They expect you to look professional.

Thomas appears and hands Loretta his bright yellow Walkman.

>   THOMAS
> Here, Mama. Listen to this on the way to the store.

Loretta puts on the headphones, listens, then grimaces.

>   LORETTA
>   *(removes headphones)*
> What *is* this . . . ?

>   THOMAS
> It's a pos'tive thinkin' tape.
>   *(off her look)*
> If you keep sayin' it, you can *do* it!

>   ROSA LYNN
> You just be sure to put that thing away when they're
> talkin' to you.

Seeing Tracy eye her from her cage, Loretta eases closer.

>   LORETTA
> What you lookin' at, Tracy? Don't you even recognize
> your own Mama . . . ?

Tracy shrieks and lunges. Loretta yelps but recovers with laughter, joined by Thomas. Tracy leers and howls.

> LORETTA
>
> You got it, girl! I ain't gonna take no for an answer this time!
>
> *(opens the door)*
>
> Well, wish me luck. . . .

> THOMAS
>
> G'luck, Mama!

> ROSA LYNN
>
> Now you be sure to call me, the *very minute* you get that job!

EXT. SHOPPING DISTRICT — DAY

Loretta jauntily walks along, headphones on, looking a little sheepish as she repeats, apparently with the Walkman:

> LORETTA
>
> I can *do* it! . . . I can *do* it! . . .

INT. GROCERY MANAGER'S BOOTH — DAY

Loretta sits, nervous, across from the MANAGER, who appraises her skeptically: overdressed, Walkman, headphones-as-necklace.

> MANAGER
>
> The job pays minimum wage. If you're lucky enough to get in thirty hours, you'll take home about a hundred ten a week.
>
> *(pulls paper from a drawer)*
>
> And the first time you don't show up, you're outta here. OK, one last thing . . .
>
> *(hands her the paper)*

                          MANAGER
A basic math test, just to make sure you know your
dollars and cents.

                          LORETTA
                   (stares, and stammers)
I thought the machine did all the figurin'. . . .

                          MANAGER
Most of the time. But sometimes it breaks down, and
the checkout clerk has to do things manually.
                   (shrewdly eyes her)
Ms. Sinclair, what's five dollars minus three dollars and
eighty-seven cents?

*Loretta blankly stares. Trembling, she stands and exits, but she's immediately
back.*

                          LORETTA
Isn't there *somethin'* I can do? Put stuff on the shelves,
mop the floors?
                   (eyes pleading)
Anything at all . . . ?

Off his silence, she turns away.

EXT. GROCERY STORE—DAY

*Loretta leans against a wall to fight back tears, collect her dignity and regain
her breath.*

EXT. STREET—DAY

*Loretta aimlessly wanders. Waiting at a light, she puts on the headphones.
Seeing something, she tugs them back down.*

WHAT SHE SEES: Right across the street is a liquor store.

She takes a very deep breath, crosses her arms and stares.

EXT. PARK PLAYGROUND—DAY

Filled with happy, squealing kids at play.
Loretta watches from a distant bench, sipping from a small bottle wrapped in a
paper bag. When a particularly delighted squeal draws her attention, she lowers
the bottle.

WHAT SHE SEES: A smiling Young Mother gently swings a Toddler, but this
one's happy and healthy and full of life.

Loretta glumly raises the bottle to her lips.

EXT. COURTYARD DRIVE—DAY

A little drunk, Loretta passes by Marco, parked with his usual entourage. Off
his smile, she lowers her headphones.

> MARCO
>
> Hey, Loretta.

> LORETTA
> *(half-heartedly)*
>
> Hey, Marco.

> MARCO
> *(shrewd appraisal)*
>
> You sure look like you feelin' good.

> LORETTA
>
> Somethin' like that.

> MARCO
>
> You know I always got a little party goin' on. . . .

> LORETTA
> *(shakes her head)*
>
> I'm in 'nough trouble as it is.

MARCO

You got somethin' better to do?

LORETTA

Got no money, anyway.

MARCO

That's OK, we'll work somethin' out when you're feelin'
a little better.
(tempting smile)
It'll make you forget your troubles for a while. . . .

Loretta considers, then shrugs. Marco says something we can't hear to an
impossibly young — maybe five or six? — "lieutenant," who nods his
understanding.

Taking Loretta's hand, he almost skips as he leads her away.

INT. APARTMENT — DAY

Rosa Lynn bounces Tracy on her knee while avoiding the child's sharp
fingernails. She brightens when she hears a key in the lock. When Thomas
enters, she eases Tracy down.

ROSA LYNN

You need to watch Tracy for awhile.

THOMAS
(guarded)

She get the job?

ROSA LYNN

I don't know.

THOMAS

She call from the store?

ROSA LYNN
(opens the door)
You just play with Tracy till I get home.

EXT./INT. GROCERY — DAY

Seen through the grate-protected plate glass, Rosa Lynn gives the hapless manager a piece of her mind.

EXT. COURTYARD ENTRANCE — DAY

Rosa Lynn passes Marco's entourage. Eyeing his wicked smile, she tries to make herself be heard above his pounding music.

ROSA LYNN
You seen Loretta?

She glares at Marco, who stands in his car seat with a grin and, to the amusement of his crew, dances in place. He reaches down to the dash and the music abruptly stops.

MARCO
(mock pain)
Whatsa matter, Miss Rosa? You don't like my music?
(off her glare)
Well, if you don't like it so much, then I won't make
you listen to it.

He now displays the yellow Walkman like a trophy. With exaggerated care, he puts on the headphones and starts to silently dance. His smile is evil; his silent dance, grotesque.

As Rosa Lynn turns and marches off in the direction Loretta was led, Marco calls out to a passing boy:

MARCO
Hey! Little Man! . . . You wanna earn yourself a dope-
fresh new Walk-Man?

INT. APARTMENT BUILDING CORRIDOR—DAY

A dank, endless, grafitti-and-trash-strewn tunnel. Sounds of music, TV or an argument waft from beyond various doors.

The fire door creaks open and Rosa Lynn enters from the stairwell, damp and breathing hard. She recovers briefly against the wall but marches on, her eyes set dead ahead.

INT. CRACK DEN KITCHEN AREA—DAY

Perched on the warped counter, Loretta drinks from a can of beer. An EMACIATED WOMAN offers a hit from her crack pipe.

> LORETTA
> *(shakes her head)*
> Start in with that stuff, ain't no turnin' back.

> EMACIATED WOMAN
> Now, how you know that, if you won't even try it?

When Loretta again shakes her head, the emaciated woman shrugs, lights a flame and raises the pipe to her own lips.

> EMACIATED WOMAN
> It's soooo sweet, the sweetest thing you'll ever have. . . .

Loretta jolts when the door buzzer erupts and never stops. The emaciated woman heads towards sweet oblivion.

> EMACIATED WOMAN
> Don't worry 'bout it, they go away. . . .

But Loretta seems to recognize the harshness of that buzz.

INT. APARTMENT BUILDING CORRIDOR—DAY

Rosa Lynn keeps her finger hard to the buzzer and glares directly at the peephole. A sudden eruption inside:

MALE VOICE 1 (OS)

Somebody get that door!

(long beat)

I said *Get . . . that . . . DOOR!*

FEMALE VOICE (OS)

(overlapping shriek)

Don't you touch me, don't you *ever* touch me!

MALE VOICE 2 (OS)

(screams through the door)

She ain't here!

(Rosa Lynn presses)

Get outta here, old woman, she *ain't here!*

(continues over)

Rosa Lynn presses until the escalating buzzing/shrieking seem to blow the door right open.

INT. BUILDING CORRIDOR/CRACK DEN—DAY

Cautiously peering inside, Rosa Lynn is taken aback.

WHAT SHE SEES: The same layout as her own apartment, but with the barest hodgepodge of ratty "furniture." Sheets tacked over the windows block out the sunlight.

Through dim and smoky haze, bodies lounge about on moldy mattresses—one COUPLE fondles, another shares a pipe.

ROSA LYNN

Loretta?! . . .

(no response)

Don't you make me come in there after you!

(no response)

Loretta, *please* . . .

Now her shock melts into utter dismay.

WHAT SHE SEES: Loretta stands in the kitchen area, defiantly smiling as she displays what appears to be her crack pipe.

The two women lock eyes. Their stand-off is broken by the loud, wet sounds of a Man urinating in the open bathroom. Loretta snickers. Rosa Lynn turns away.

INT. APARTMENT BUILDING CORRIDOR — DAY

Rosa Lynn now walks in slow defeat. Loretta's distant laughter grows maniacal before ending with a door's slam.

INT. ROSA LYNN'S APARTMENT — DAY

Tracy's on the floor like a frozen Buddha, her face that of an inhuman automaton. Thomas squats there with her tiger, tempting her with all the green money "stuffed" inside.

THOMAS
See, Tracy? Made 'nother six dollars today. Pretty soon we gonna have 'nough to buy new TV.

He zips up the tiger's back, then props it on Tracy's rigid lap, but it topples off. Frustrated, he tries picking her up.

THOMAS
C'mon, Tracy . . .

Tracy arches and emits a room-swallowing shriek. He lets go.

THOMAS
Whoa, OK, sorry, you got it . . .

Upon Rosa Lynn's grim entrance, he immediately withdraws.

THOMAS
You find her?

> ROSA LYNN
> *(avoids his gaze)*

Uh-huh.

Thomas walks toward his room, but pauses.

> THOMAS

She still got my Walkman?

> ROSA LYNN
> *(shrugs)*

Prob'ly with the TV by now.

Thomas stares at the tiger on the floor. Fighting back tears, he slams his hand against the wall.

> THOMAS

Damn! Why she always got to go do that?! Seem like ev'rytime we get somethin', she find a way to mess it up!

> ROSA LYNN
> *(weakly)*

She's not herself, Thomas. . . .

Thomas runs toward his room.

> THOMAS

She *nothin'!*

His bedroom door slams. Rosa Lynn eases into her rocker and and picks up a nearby framed photograph and sadly studies it.

WHAT SHE SEES: It looks like a Sears family portrait, where a beaming Rosa Lynn's arm is linked with that of a very pregnant and smiling Loretta. Loretta's hand cradles the head of a younger Thomas, whose own ear is pressed against her swollen belly.

Rosa Lynn lowers the photograph to stare at the motionless, emotionless Tracy, still on the floor.

LATER, SAME LOCATION

As day turns to dusk, Rosa Lynn slowly rocks and cradles her Bible. Tracy is slumped over where we saw her, asleep.

Rosa Lynn opens the Bible to retrieve the memorable envelope holding Earl's letter, unfolds it for reference, then picks up the phone. She hesitates before dialing, then:

> ROSA LYNN
>
> Hello, Earl? . . . It's Rosa Lynn.

EXT. MISSISSIPPI COUNTRYSIDE — MAGIC HOUR

Pine trees, pastures, ponds of still waters, all bathed in fading light. We might recognize this as the setting of our opening scenes, perhaps.

> ROSA LYNN (OS)
>
> Earl . . . ?

> EARL (OS)
> *(long pause)*
>
> I'm right here.

> ROSA LYNN (OS)
>
> I got your letter.

> EARL (OS)
> *(noncommitally)*
>
> Uh-huh.

> ROSA LYNN (OS)
>
> Earl . . . It's time to talk.

INT. EARL'S LIVING ROOM — EVENING

A little later. Seated in a big chair by the fireplace, EARL SINCLAIR is age seventy and annoyed.

> ### EARL
> *(into the phone)*
> *No*, Rosa Lynn, you listen to *me* . . .
> *(instead listens)*
> I don't care if she is my niece, I haven't seen her since her father died, so you know better'n askin' me to take 'em in like that. Besides, me and Annie's too old to be runnin' around after little kids all day long. You got any idea how wild a three-year-old can be?

INTERCUT WITH:

INT. ROSA LYNN'S APARTMENT — EVENING

Rosa Lynn can't help but smile at the temporarily harmless, sleeping Tracy. All patient reasoning:

> ### ROSA LYNN
> Earl Sinclair, I know you've never forgiven me for burying Clayton up here instead of in the family cemetery down in the Delta. But we're talking blood family here. Your own brother's daughter, and she needs your help.

INT. EARL'S LIVING ROOM — EVENING

> ### EARL
> *(sly smile)*
> You gonna send Nathan with 'em?

> ### ROSA LYNN (OS)
> *(explosive sputter)*
> I most certainly am *not!*

EARL

Nathan belongs right here, Rosa Lynn, right here in this house! He never shoulda been kidnapped to Chicago in the first place!

INT. ROSA LYNN'S LIVING ROOM—EVENING

ROSA LYNN
(scoffs)

Oh, he was not kidnapped, Earl, and you know the family tradition. Nathan gets passed down from oldest child to oldest child, so he stays right here until Thomas comes of age. And Earl?
(turns ominous)
If it comes down to it . . . I'll *sell* Nathan if I have to.
(off Earl's sputters)
If I have to choose between savin' Nathan and savin' my family, you *know* what I'll choose!

INT. EARL'S LIVING ROOM—EVENING

Earl's mind is racing.

ROSA LYNN (OS)

Don't . . . Make . . . Me . . . *Choose,* Earl.

EARL
(caves)

Oh, all right, Rosa Lynn.
(recovers)
But only for the summer, you understand? And they gotta stay real quiet 'round Annie, she's too old to put up with no nonsense!

INT. ROSA LYNN'S LIVING ROOM—EVENING

Victory achieved, Rosa Lynn smiles and settles back.

ROSA LYNN

Yes, I understand, and they will, too.
(all *sweetness* now)
Oh, and Earl? You know how you used to breed
huntin' dogs and all? You don't happen to have any of
those big ol' cages around, do you?
(She again *ponders* Tracy, who *twitches* in her *sleep*.)
No, no . . . No special reason. Just askin' . . .
(pause, then gently)
And Earl? . . . Thank you.

INT. EARL'S LIVING ROOM — EVENING

Earl hangs up, contemplating, then looks around and stands.

EARL

Annie . . . ?

INT. EARL'S ENTRANCE HALL — EVENING

*Earl finds 69-year-old ANNIE mumbling in frustration at the closed front door.
He addresses her in a soothing lilt:*

EARL

No, no, no . . .

*He gently takes her hand in his to point to the hand-lettered sign taped on the
door: NO NO NO.*

EARL

No, no, no . . .
(off her blank stare)
No, no, no . . .

ANNIE
(backs away, mumbling)

No, no, no . . .

EARL

That's right. . . . No, no, no . . .

Annie allows Earl to gently lead her from the door.

INT. EARL'S LIVING ROOM—EVENING

Earl helps Annie sit, and places a rag doll in her hands. Her eyes vacant as Tracy's, she softly sings:

ANNIE

No, no, no . . . No, no, no . . .

INT. ROSA LYNN'S LIVING ROOM—NIGHT

Dark as we hear locks turn. The door opens and Loretta enters and turns on a light, startled to find Rosa Lynn rocking in the dark. Loretta's voice is a ragged whisper:

LORETTA

I know, I know . . . We got to talk.

ROSA LYNN
(weary but firm)

I'm done talkin', Loretta. Done talkin' forever. I can't
raise your children, and they can't raise themselves.
Now you gonna do *exactly* as I tell you, or I'm callin'
Child Welfare in the mornin'.

Loretta moves towards the bathroom, but stops at the sight of Thomas in his briefs, who stands there and stares. Finally:

LORETTA

I'm sorry, baby.

THOMAS
(stares; softly)

Ain't that much sorry in the world, Mama.

He turns into his room and silently closes the door.

EXT. SHOPPING DISTRICT — DAY

Loretta keeps pace with Rosa Lynn, equipped with her canvas shopping bag. Thomas "walks" Tracy via a leash attached to her chest harness. When they cross paths with a dog being similarly walked, each creature strains for the other.

>   ROSA LYNN
> . . . And down in the Delta, there's great big fields to run and play in, and nobody chasin' after you but your own shadow.

>   LORETTA
> Them fields are fulla *snakes*, Thomas! *Big* snakes! They got more kindsa snakes'n we got rats!

>   THOMAS
>   (to Rosa Lynn, worried)
> They really got lotsa snakes down there?

>   ROSA LYNN
> Oh, don't you listen to her. She's just mad 'cause it's a dry county. Besides, if you don't wanna play in the fields, you can learn how to swim.

LORETTA

They even got snakes that can swim!

Rosa Lynn stops in front of a shop, and Loretta looks at it in surprise.

LORETTA

What're we doin' at *this* place?

ROSA LYNN
(opens the door)

We gettin' money for the bus tickets.

INT. PAWN SHOP — DAY

Rosa Lynn could well be entering the devil's sanctum, and even Loretta appears uneasy. But Thomas gazes about in awe.

WHAT THEY SEE: All kinds of guns. Behind the Plexiglas partition, shotguns and assault rifles are mounted on the wall. Under the counter, handguns gleam in all shapes and sizes.

The huge, lumbering PAWNBROKER looks capable of handling any of the weapons. She's friendly, though:

PAWNBROKER

Hey, Loretta . . . You got somethin' for me today?

Loretta winces. Rosa Lynn gives her a withering look, then shrewdly appraises the pawnbroker.

ROSA LYNN

I *might* have somethin'. . . .

She looks to confirm that nobody else is in the shop, then slowly draws a cloth bundle from her bag.

She meticulously unwraps it to reveal an elaborately designed and exquisitely crafted, three-pronged, ANTIQUE SILVER CANDELABRA.

Loretta's eyes widen and she reverently breathes one word:

> LORETTA
>
> Nathan . . .

The pawnbroker's small intrigued smile evaporates into a poker face as she and Rosa Lynn square off.

> PAWNBROKER
> *(disinterested sniff)*
> Silver plate, maybe worth a hundred fifty.

> ROSA LYNN
> Solid sterling. Nothing less than five hundred dollars.

> PAWNBROKER
> Can't be any older'n nineteen fifties. . . . Maybe go as high as two hundred. Maybe.

Rosa Lynn moves the candelabra closer and turns it enticingly.

> ROSA LYNN
> Antique silver, I'll have you know. Eighteen fifty-two. Look close, here on the bottom . . . Silversmith-signed and engraved-dated.

Rosa Lynn presses the flat bottom squarely against the plexiglas on her side. The pawnbroker presses a jeweler's glass against her side and squints into it.

> LORETTA
> Where's he been all these years?

> ROSA LYNN
> He's been under safe lock and key at the church.

The pawnbroker straightens.

ROSA LYNN

Easily worth four hundred and fifty.

PAWNBROKER

American. Three hundred.

ROSA LYNN

British. Four.

PAWNBROKER

All right, three fifty. Final offer.
(deadpan)
Or you might try Sotheby's. But I don't know if they're
open on Saturdays.

ROSA LYNN

Three seventy-five, and it's done.

PAWNBROKER
(beat, terse nod)

Done.

The Pawnbroker counts green bills from a huge wad of cash.

PAWNBROKER

Twenty, forty, sixty, eighty . . .

Thomas inquisitively tries to follow the conversation:

LORETTA

You *can't* do this. Nathan's too important. . . .

ROSA LYNN

More important than *what*, Loretta? What's the point of
savin' Nathan for the next generation, when the next
generation isn't gonna be there?

PAWNBROKER

Hundred sixty . . . Hundred eighty . . .

LORETTA

But he's been in the family forever. . . .

ROSA LYNN

And he can *stay* in the family, too! It's all up to you.

The pawnbroker places a ticket atop the stack of green bills on her side of the turntable, ready to make the transaction.

PAWNBROKER

Three hundred seventy-five dollars. You got till
September the fifth.

Loretta's eyes make one last pleading attempt, but Rosa Lynn turns to Thomas.

ROSA LYNN

You remember to bring that camera?

THOMAS
(removes his knapsack)

Yes, ma'am.

ROSA LYNN
(to Loretta)

You hear that? You got till September fifth to make
'nough money to get yourself back home and rescue
Nathan.

She smiles and proudly displays Nathan for the Polaroid's flash. She places Nathan on the turntable, caresses him good-bye, then signals her readiness. The turntable swivels until Nathan and the cash trade sides.

ROSA LYNN
(counts the money)

You take good care of my Nathan, now.
(puts the money down her blouse)

We'll be back with your money.

The pawnbroker admires her gleaming prize.

PAWNBROKER

I hope not.
                    (*satisfied smile*)
This'll melt down *real* nice. . . .

EXT. PAWNSHOP — DAY

Exiting, Rosa Lynn tries to give Loretta the pawn ticket.

ROSA LYNN

Here. This belongs to you.

LORETTA
(*shakes her head*)
I ain't gonna take it.

Rosa Lynn's look and tone are equally flat:

ROSA LYNN

Fine.

She stalks right over to a litter barrel, drops the ticket in and marches away without looking back.

ROSA LYNN

Come on, Thomas. We have to go buy the bus tickets.

Thomas briefly looks to Loretta, but drags Tracy to catch up. Rosa Lynn grips Thomas's hand. Calmly, with her eyes fixed ahead:

ROSA LYNN

And don't you *even* look back.

Loretta at first stubbornly watches their departing backs, but eventually stomps over and angrily fishes in the trash.

INT. BUS TERMINAL — NIGHT

At the side of a big Greyhound, Rosa Lynn and Loretta watch the burly DRIVER slide a large, flat box into the cargo bin.

ROSA LYNN

Now you be sure to call me, collect, when you're changin' buses in Memphis.

LORETTA
(aloof)

Uh-huh.

Rosa Lynn trails after her to the door of the bus.

ROSA LYNN

You eat *only* the food I packed for you. Don't you take any food from strangers.

Thomas waits at the door, holding Tracy back on her leash with one hand, the stuffed tiger with the other. A boarding PASSENGER looks askance at this dubious combination.

ROSA LYNN

You be sure to show your Uncle Earl respect. And be extra nice to Aunt Annie, she's gettin' a little slow, you know.

Rosa Lynn turns to Thomas and Tracy. She caresses his head, then stiffly bends to collectively hug them.

THOMAS
(glum muffle)

Bye, Gramma . . .

ROSA LYNN
(hand lingering)

Don't you look so down. Why, you gonna have such a nice summer and you'll be home before you know it.

Thomas attempts a smile and, hefting Tracy, boards the bus.

Loretta wants to board, but Rosa Lynn stands firmly between her and the door, appraising her with a confident smile.

Loretta. Daughter.
>   (*arms reaching out*)
I . . . want . . . you . . .
>   (*smile broadens*)
To have a *wonderful* journey!

She hugs Loretta, who is at first unresponsive but then returns the hug, silently but genuinely. Loretta turns, takes a breath and steps up into the bus.

Remembering, Rosa Lynn reverts to form, calling up after her:

ROSA LYNN

And you make sure you give Earl that picture, you hear me?

The door's about to close, but she abruptly clambers aboard.

INT. BUS—NIGHT

Rosa Lynn peers down the dark aisle.

ROSA LYNN

And don't you say *anything* 'bout Nathan bein' in a
pawn shop!

(off silence)

You hear me?!

LORETTA (OS)

(from the back)

Yeah, yeah, I hear you, I hear you, the whole damn
world hears you!

(plaintively)

Can we please go now?

Rosa Lynn gives the bemused driver a brusque nod and exits.

INT. BUS STATION — NIGHT

*The door hisses shut. Rosa Lynn finds their window and waves. Thomas moves
Tracy's hand to wave back, then wrestles her away from the window to keep her
from breaking the glass. As the bus pulls away, Passengers' expressions indicate
that Tracy's wail is already at high pitch, as we . . .*

GO TO BLACK.

EXT. MARIANNA, MISSISSIPPI — DAY

*A sleepier version of Mayberry, now fallen on hard times: A weedy town square
with a chipped Civil War monument. A few stores, several boarded shut. Few
people about.*

INT. PERCY'S FURNITURE MART — DAY

*A banner promotes a going out of business sale, but there are no customers. Earl
speaks urgently to PERCY:*

EARL

Percy, if you shut down, we'll have to go all the way to
Clarksdale to buy our new sofa.

PERCY
(deadpan)
You been talkin' about that new sofa for the last five
years, Earl. Take it from me, *now's* the time to buy.

EXT. COMBO GAS/BUS STATION—DAY

*As the bus approaches, Earl leans against his car and grimly toys with his huge
ring of keys, tuning out the whines of an elderly PRIM WOMAN.*

PRIM WOMAN
It was bad 'nough they cut service back to three days a
week, but now I hear the closest stop's gonna be way
over in Yazoo City.
(*as the bus pulls in*)
Now how's Sister gonna come visit me, if she can't even
get here?

*Against the sounds of Tracy's wails, PRIM SISTER practically bolts from the
bus, dressed as though she were disembarking from the Queen Mary on Easter.
The sisters share a brief hug.*

PRIM WOMAN
Sister! . . . How was your trip? You must be so
tired. . . .

PRIM SISTER
Just get me outta here!
(*they start walking*)
You wouldn't believe the kindsa trash they're lettin' on
buses nowadays! . . .

*Thomas steps down, shielding his eyes from the sun and clutching the tiger.
Loretta appears, tugging out the howling, leashed Tracy.*

LORETTA
What you cryin' about?!
(*light tug*)
C'mon now, get on outta there!

She casts a dark look at the departing Prim Sister, then turns to Earl.

LORETTA

You Uncle Earl?

From Earl's expression, he wishes he weren't.

WHAT HE SEES: Loretta, scowling; Tracy, howling on her leash; Thomas, clutching the Tiger.

Loretta's own appraisal is equally unenthusiastic.

WHAT SHE SEES: With those jangling keys and dour expression, Earl could be a prison guard, just waiting to haul them away.

LATER, SAME LOCATION

Earl and Loretta now strain to heft the huge, flat box into the trunk of Earl's car.

EARL

What's in here, anyway?

LORETTA

Tracy's crib.

EARL
(catches his breath)
A big girl like that's still sleepin' in a crib?
(crouches to baby-talk to Tracy)
Huh? Now what's a big girl like you doin', still sleepin'
in a crib?

Tracy shrieks and lunges for his face. Earl jumps back.

LORETTA
(matter of factly)
Oh, don't you worry 'bout that, she does it all the time.
Just never look her right in the eyes like that. . . .
(slams the trunk shut)
Makes her crazy.

INT. EARL'S CAR—DAY

Loretta notices that her inside passenger door handle has been removed. Starting the engine:

> EARL
>
> That's so Annie won't try to get out when I'm drivin'.

Loretta's eyes are still wide off the missing handle, when we hear the sudden "thunk!" of the electronic doorlocks accompany the abrupt "shwoop!" of the shoulder belt closing across her. She yelps and shoots Earl an accusing look.

INT./EXT. EARL'S CAR—DAY

On the meandering drive out of town, Earl, making the most of his meager assets, sounds like a one-man Chamber of Commerce. He indicates a storefront next to one that's boarded shut.

> EARL
>
> That's a health clinic, where the old five-and-dime used to be. A doctor from Greenway comes over twice a week.

> LORETTA
> *(no interest)*
>
> Uh-huh . . .

Earl indicates a boarded-up school building.

> EARL
>
> That's the old high school. It closed after the white folks started sendin' their kids to the private school. We're tryin' to get 'nough money together to turn it into a community center.

> LORETTA
> *(some interest)*
>
> Uh-*huh*. You gonna have pool tables?

EARL

(ignores that)

That's my restaurant.

"Just Chicken" looks like a converted Dairy Queen. On its roof is a huge, crude, two-dimensional cut-out of a chicken's head, its mechanized beak irregularly creaking open and closed.

EARL

I started it after I retired from the chicken plant.

LORETTA

(great interest)

You serve beer there?

EARL

(ignores that, too)

That there's the chicken plant.

Southern Pride Poultry, a sad clump of old Butler buildings.

EARL

Worked there thirty years. It's 'bout the only big piece of business around, ever since they shut down the blue-jeans mill.

EXT./INT. EARL'S CAR—DAY

Meandering along a country road, Earl honks at a pond where two men are wading. They look over and wave.

THOMAS

What they doin'?

EARL

That's a catfish farm. Those men are out there feeding the catfish they're growing.

THOMAS
(*dubious stare*)
Ain't they scared 'bout snakes?

INT./EXT. EARL'S CAR—DAY

They turn onto a gravel drive.

EARL
Here we are.

Loretta raises her eyebrows in surprise.

WHAT SHE SEES: A large, old, two-story farmhouse—nothing like a Tara-style columned mansion, but with a big front porch. It sits on a small rise of green lawn.

THOMAS
Whoa . . . It's big.

EARL
(*eyes with pride*)
It's an old plantation house, built right before the Civil War.

LORETTA
You born here?

EARL
(*dryly*)
Yeah, but not in the house.

Earl parks his new sedan next to an old, dented Toyota.

EXT. EARL'S HOUSE—DAY

They step from the car.

> EARL

All this used to be owned by the white Sinclairs, but the last of 'em died out fifty years ago. I bought it in seventy-two, a real mess by then.
>> *(eyes the house with pride)*

Been fixin' it up ever since.
>> *(points to nearby fields)*

See them fields? Your parents and I used to pick cotton in them fields when we were little kids.

> LORETTA

You don't still pick cotton, do you?

> EARL
>> *(chuckles)*

Not if I can help it. A big company owns all the land 'round here, and they use machines to pick the cotton.
>> *(heads for the porch)*

C'mon inside, we'll get your things in a minute. I want y'all to meet your Aunt Annie and Zenia.

EXT. FRONT PORCH—DAY

At the closed door, Earl searches on his big key ring.

> LORETTA

Who's Zenia?

> EARL

She's our caregiver.

> LORETTA
>> *(mutters)*

Just call a maid, a *maid*. . . .

INT. FRONT HALLWAY—DAY

Earl closes the door, then firmly locks them all inside, just below the hand-lettered sign that says NO NO NO. *Loretta and Thomas exchange warning looks.*

EARL

C'mon back. Bet they're in the kitchen.

LORETTA

Which way's the bathroom?

EARL
(points)
That open door at the end of the hall.

LORETTA
(hesitates)
Do I need a key to get in?

EARL

No . . .
(she starts toward it)
None of the inside doors even have locks on 'em.

Loretta jolts and moves on, but with a real sinking feeling.

INT. LIVING ROOM—DAY

Thomas follows Earl. As he tries to keep Tracy from tearing away, he takes in all the comfort promised by this room.

INT. KITCHEN—DAY

ZENIA, in her mid-30s, looks up from cutting vegetables at the counter, with a strangely fixed, too-pleasant smile.

EARL

Zenia, this is my great-nephew, Thomas.

Big knife poised, she greets Thomas with her smile and a too-measured-and-pleasant, Stepford-like demeanor and tone:

ZENIA

Hello, Thomas. How are you?

• 45 •

THOMAS
(gulps, stares)
Fine. I guess. Ma'am.

EARL
This is Tracy.

Tracy squirms on her leash. Zenia's eyes narrow, just a bit.

EARL
And this is your Aunt Annie.

Thomas turns, and his eyes widen.

WHAT HE SEES: Annie seated at the table, mumbling as she laboriously sorts mixed coins into different jars.

EARL
(pecks her cheek)
You been a good girl today, Annie?

ANNIE
(agitated)
No, no, no . . . Get this right . . .

INT. BATHROOM—DAY

Loretta hikes her skirt, drops her pants and sits, coming face to face with a hand-lettered sign taped to the wall: "Wipe Yourself. Flush."

INT. KITCHEN—DAY

Thomas's eyes dart from Annie to Tracy, then back to Annie.

THOMAS
Wha's wrong with her?

EARL
(follows his darting eyes)

It's called Alzheimer's disease. It happens to some people when they get old. They just slow down more than other people.

Tracy has calmed down enough to stare — with intrigue? — at Annie.

INT. LIVING ROOM — DAY

Huddled in a corner with the phone, Loretta speaks low and fast.

LORETTA

I'm tellin' you, he's *crazy!* . . . He thinks he's some kinda prison guard or somethin'! . . . Uh-huh. First he locked us in the car, now he got locked us in the house, and he got signs *ev'rywhere*, tellin' you what to do and. . .

Glancing up to see Earl's looming, puzzled presence, she yelps and drops the phone.

INT. KITCHEN — DAY

Thomas observes Annie sort her coins.

THOMAS

She always like this?

ZENIA

Oh, no . . . She's got her good days and her bad days.
(pats Annie's shoulder)
This is just one of your quiet days, huh, Miss Annie?

As Earl leads Loretta in, she sees Annie and draws a breath.

LORETTA

Sweet Baby Jesus . . .

Annie looks up. Seeing Loretta, her expression dissolves from dazed confusion to sweet recognition.

ANNIE

Mama . . .

Loretta looks at Earl, who smiles.

EARL

It's OK. She does this all the time, mistakin' people.
Tomorrow, she might just think you're Lena Horne.
Just go 'long with her.

ANNIE

Mama. . .

EARL

Go give your Aunt Annie a little hug.
                    (off Loretta's reluctance)
Go on, she won't hurt you.

Loretta stiffly bends to give Annie a very tentative hug.

INT. LIVING ROOM — NIGHT

Earl and Loretta are alone.

EARL

You ever waited on tables before?

LORETTA
(shakes her head)
I'm not too good at figurin' the bill.

EARL

Well, there's lotsa other things to do in a restaurant.
We'll find you somethin'.

Thomas enters and hands Loretta her purse.

LORETTA

She asleep yet?

THOMAS

Sorta. She still buggin' out a little.

Loretta fishes around in her bag for something. Earl observes Thomas stare the dark TV.

EARL

Only reason we have that fool thing is to keep Annie entertained. Never picked up the habit myself.

THOMAS
(wistful stare)

Me, neither.

Loretta hands Earl the Polaroid picture.

LORETTA

Mama wanted you to have this.

Earl looks at it and scowls.

WHAT HE SEES: Rosa Lynn stares directly at us, displaying her hostage.

THOMAS

Who's Nathan?

Earl eyes him quizzically.

EARL

That's what my great-grandfather, Jesse, called this candelabra.
(a beat)
Rosa Lynn never told you?

Loretta and Thomas shake their heads.

LORETTA

Just that he'd been in the family a long time, and came
up to Chicago with her and Daddy.

EARL

Huh . . . Maybe she figured you weren't ready to hear
the full Story of Nathan yet.
(considers for a beat)

EARL

Anyway, before the Civil War, my great-grandfather
Jesse was a slave, and a sharecropper after that. . .

As he continues, we FLASHBACK to illustrate his story . . .

INT. SHARECROPPER'S SHACK — 1922

A single room of hardcore rural poverty. Several SAD PEOPLE sit or stand
about, as if waiting. . . .

EARL (VO)

All his life, Jesse only had two things. A big family,
which was real important to him. And this candelabra,
which he called Nathan.

A dying OLD MAN is in the bed. A SAD MAN sits there in vigil, with the old
man's hand in one of his own, the candelabra in the other.

EARL (VO)

When Jesse was dyin', he gave Nathan to his oldest
son. He told him that as long as Nathan stayed in the
Sinclair family, the family would stay together.

INT. EARL'S LIVING ROOM — PRESENT

Loretta and Thomas pay rapt attention.

LORETTA

And Nathan's been in the family ever since?

Passed down from my grandfather . . . to my father . . .
to your father.

(his eyes narrow)

Then when I was off at the Korean War, times were
real hard in the Delta, and Rosa Lynn talked your
father into goin' off to Chicago. They left the family
behind, and took Nathan with them.

LORETTA

Weren't lots of people movin' up to Chicago back then?

EARL

"Lots of people" didn't hafta include Nathan. And he
shoulda been sent back down anyway, after your father
died. But that woman just had to hold onto him.

LORETTA

(too evenly)

"That woman" scrubbed hospital floors and emptied
bedpans for forty years to keep things together 'nough
to hold onto him.

EARL

(appraising beat)

Yes, you certainly are her daughter . . . Anyway, I guess
it don't matter where Nathan is. Just that he's still in
the family, his spirit bein' passed along. And someday,
he'll be passed on down to you, Thomas.

*As Earl moves to prop the Polaroid up on the mantel (filling the same empty
space we remember from the opening scene), Thomas looks uneasily to Loretta,
who barely shakes her head.*

EXT. COUNTRYSIDE — MORNING

Dew on the grass, cows grazing, men and machines already at work in the fields.

EXT. FRONT PORCH — MORNING

Thomas steps out and uses the key dangling around his neck to lock the door. Ambling down the porch, he freezes.

WHAT HE SEES: Two deer stand among the bushes not more than ten feet away, looking right at us.

Thomas slowly backs away, then races for the door. There is a moment of fumbling before he remembers the key.

A LITTLE LATER

Now with his camera, Thomas creeps back like a jungle commando. Reaching the end, he peeks around the corner to see . . . nothing. The deer are gone.

Earl walks out, annoyed at finding the front door left open.

> EARL
>
> What you doin' out here?

> THOMAS
> *(wonderment)*
> I saw some wild animals . . . I think they were deer, but I ain't 'xactly sure.

> EARL
> *(softens)*
> They prob'ly were deer. They like to come out early enough to eat up my good bushes.
> *(they walk inside)*
> You gotta remember now 'bout keepin' that door locked, even if you're comin' out for just a minute, you understand?

INT. FRONT HALLWAY — MORNING

Earl locks the door behind them.

EARL

Go on upstairs and tell your mama to hurry it up. It's
almost time to leave for the restaurant.

INT. LORETTA'S BEDROOM—MORNING

*Thomas finds Loretta still asleep, the alarm clutched in her hand. Tracy's asleep
in her crib-cage, clutching her tiger.*

THOMAS

Mama?

LORETTA
(groggy)

Get outta here. . . .

THOMAS

Uncle Earl's 'bout ready to take off for the restaurant,
and he say ten miles an awful long way to walk. . . .

She bolts upright.

INT. KITCHEN—MORNING

*Annie and Earl are at the table. Annie abruptly drops her small triangle of toast,
stands and paces in frustration.*

EARL

Annie, what do you want?
(she stops)
What you lookin' for?

ANNIE

What time is it?

EARL
(stands)

Well, let's go see.

He leads her to the counter, where the digital clock boldly reads 7:22. He uses her hand to point to its dial.

> EARL
> Here we go. It's se-ven twen-ty-two.
> *(a beat)*
> It's se-ven twen-ty-two. . . .

Annie just stares at the clock.

INT. FRONT HALLWAY — MORNING

Loretta hurries down the stairs in the same good dress she wore job hunting. Zenia enters the front door, and offers a Stepford smile and chirp.

> ZENIA
> Good morrrr-ning!

> LORETTA
> *(a little spooked)*
> Uhm, yeah . . . right.

INT. KITCHEN — MORNING

Still at the clock, Annie's finally got it.

> ANNIE AND EARL
> It's se-ven twen-ty-three . . .
> *(beat)*
> It's se-ven twen-ty-three . . .

> ANNIE
> *(looks up brightly)*
> When do we eat?

Loretta bursts in, and freezes when Annie stares at her. Annie points at the clock.

> ANNIE
> It's se-ven twen-ty-three . . .

LORETTA
(thrown)
OK, OK, so I overslept a little. . . . *Shoot* me.

LATER, SAME LOCATION

Now full and active.

Annie "helps" Zenia by endlessly drying one plate as though polishing it. At the table, Earl warily eyes Thomas snatch the jelly from Tracy's reach.

EARL
Now what's your job gonna be?

THOMAS
(without enthusiasm)
Look after Tracy.

EARL
You keep her 'way from your Aunt Annie, now.
(to Annie, sing-song)
Bye-bye . . . Bye-bye, Annie.

ANNIE
(confused)
Bye-bye? . . .

Earl gives her a little kiss on the cheek.

EARL
That's right . . . Bye-bye . . . Bye-bye.

As Annie smiles and repeats, Zenia joins their chorus.

ZENIA
That's right . . . Bye-bye . . .

Earl motions for Thomas and Loretta to join. Thomas finds it fun; Loretta, silly. Tracy just stares at Annie. Smiling and waving, Earl and Loretta back out the door.

> EVERYBODY
> Bye-bye . . . Bye-bye . . .

Now Zenia, Annie, Thomas and Tracy stare at each other. Tracy sends a spoon flying across the room, and we hear something break. Off Tracy's howl of glee:

> ANNIE
> Bye-bye!Bye-bye!Bye-bye! . . .

Zenia takes a deep breath to recover her smile. To Thomas:

> ZENIA
> Tell you what. I'll keep *mine* in here. You keep *yours* . . .
> (*firm point towards the living room*)
> In there.

INT. EARL'S CAR—DAY

> LORETTA
> How long she been like that? . . . Aunt Annie.

> EARL
> Oh, I guess I started seein' little things five or six years ago. At first, she kept forgettin' where she left the car keys. Eventually, she forgot what the keys were for.

> LORETTA
> (*absorbs that*)
> Maybe she should be in a home someplace.

> EARL
> (*a beat*)
> She *is* in a home.

INT. LIVING ROOM—DAY

Thomas keeps Tracy from tearing it apart. When she randomly grabs the TV's remote control, he snatches it from her.

> THOMAS
>
> Oh, no you don't . . .

He distracts her by using it, and the TV comes on.

> THOMAS
>
> Looka there, Tracy!

Tracy stares as Geraldo poses a probing question to a cross-dresser. Thomas feigns amazement.

> THOMAS
>
> Uh-huh, isn't that somethin'?

But after a moment, Tracy's whining and heading off again. Thomas works the remote, and Big Bird makes her stop again.

> THOMAS
>
> Whoa, looka that. . . .

But she's immediately restless. Thomas works the remote.

> THOMAS
>
> Look, Tracy!

As Thomas keeps pressing the remote to find something acceptable to her, she sits down on the floor to watch the changing screens—this is what she wants to do?

> THOMAS
>
> No way . . .

With a resigned sigh, he settles back in a comfortable chair, his arm stiffly extended towards the channel-surfing TV.

INT. "JUST CHICKEN" RESTAURANT—DAY

Overflowing with all sorts of chicken-themed memorabilia.

Two waitresses, GINA and ISABELLE, prep the empty restaurant.

> GINA
>
> So what'd you do?

> ISABELLE
> *(indignant)*
>
> I did what *any* self-respectin' woman in my position
> would do! I looked him right in the eye and told him,
> "Baby, if you can't give me the *re-spect* I deserve, then
> you just haul yourself back to your wife!"

*One wall is painted with a crude mural of Marianna's square, but populated by
anthropomorphic chickens, erect in halos and clothing. A caption reads:
AND THE CHICKEN SHALL INHERIT THE EARTH.*

> ISABELLE
>
> Let *her* be the one to look after you for a change. . . .

> GINA
>
> Um-hmm . . . I hear that.

Earl and Loretta enter.

> GINA & ISABELLE
>
> Mornin', Earl. . . .

> EARL
>
> Mornin'. This is Loretta, my niece I was tellin' you
> about. She's gonna be workin' with us for the summer.
> That's Gina . . . and Isabelle.

Loretta seems awkward and aloof as they exchange hellos.

INT. RESTAURANT KITCHEN—DAY

Now wearing a bibbed apron over her dress, Loretta watches as Earl bustles about, pulling some sort of giant food processor from a closet and placing it on a work counter.

> EARL
>
> The only kind of meat we serve here is chicken. We get
> it cheap from the plant, on account I used to work
> there.

He reaches into the adjacent refrigerator and pulls out a large bowl, filled with some sort of meaty-goop.

> EARL
>
> We're prob'ly known best for the homemade chicken
> sausages we make fresh every day.

He pulls on a pair of rubber gloves with the experienced snap!. . . snap! *of a surgeon.*

> EARL
>
> Now watch close while I show you how to make a
> sausage. OK, first thing, you put the empty casing
> here. . . .

Loretta dubiously observes his confident demonstration, especially when his hand reaches into the bowl of goop.

> EARL
>
> Then you stuff it. . . .
> (*her brows furrow*)
> Last thing, you tie it off.

Almost lovingly, he places a plump, perfectly shaped sausage down on the table, then steps back from the machine.

> EARL
>
> Here, you try it.

Loretta first fumbles in putting on her gloves, then gingerly picks up an empty sausage casing to dangle, at arm's length, what could be a huge condom. Staring down at the bowl of moist, ground chicken goop, she closes her eyes and reaches in.

INT. RESTAURANT DINING ROOM — DAY

Still prepping:

> ISABELLE
>
> What's she doing anyway, wearin' a dress like that to a place like this?

> GINA
>
> Um-hmm . . . I do hear that.

> ISABELLE
>
> I've never been up to Chi-ca-go, but I bet they don't dress up like that to wash dishes or anything.

> GINA
>
> Mm-mmm . . . No, they don't. . . .

> ISABELLE
>
> You don't think Earl's gonna put her over us, just cause she's his niece, do you?

> GINA
>
> Hmmmm . . .

INT. RESTAURANT KITCHEN — DAY

Her apron now splattered, Earl and Loretta stare down at two sausages, Earl's still perfectly symmetrical, hers more resembling a twisted balloon animal.

> EARL
>
> Well, it does takes some practice to get the hang of it. . . .

He reaches into the refrigerator to pull out bowls of different kinds of goop, identifying them as he puts them on the counter:

> EARL
>
> OK, first we gotta stuff the Crispy Cajun. . . .
> *(new bowl)*
> then we got the Sassy Salsa . . .
> *(new bowl)*
> and the Bar-B-Qued . . .

As he continues, Loretta glances into the refrigerator to see, to her dismay, at least a dozen bowls on its shelves.

INT. EARL'S LIVING ROOM—DAY

Thomas nows reads a magazine from one hand as he works the remote with the other. Annie bursts into the room, Zenia calmly following.

> ANNIE
>
> Ricky! Ricky!

> ZENIA
>
> That's right, it's time for Ricky.

Annie plops onto the couch. Zenia loads a tape into the VCR.

> ZENIA
>
> Put it on channel four and keep it there.
> *(presses a button)*
> This is the only TV she'll watch long 'nough to let me
> get the laundry done.

Over Tracy's whine, bright music begins and the TV screen etches with the black-and-white heart of "I Love Lucy." Off Tracy's growing whines, pointedly:

> ZENIA
>
> I do believe it's time we switched rooms.

INT. EARL'S KITCHEN—DAY

Thomas scrambles after Tracy, who's covered with flour.

> THOMAS
> Why you got to go do that for?
> *(she heads for the door)*
> Oh, no you don't.
> *(follows her out)*
> You get back here!

INT. LIVING ROOM—DAY

Annie absently lets the floured Tracy clamber onto her lap, mesmerized by Lucy and Ethel, who frantically shove candy into their pockets, down their blouses, into their mouths . . .

> ANNIE
> *(ecstatic whisper)*
> Ricky . . . Ricky . . .

Thomas shrugs at their momentarily peaceful coexistence.

LATER—LATE AFTERNOON

Thomas again reads while a cleaned-up Tracy sleeps on the floor. When Earl and Loretta enter, Thomas raises his eyebrows at Loretta's exhaustion and her rumpled, stained, no-longer "good" dress.

> THOMAS
> What happened to you?

> LORETTA
> *(irritated)*
> Don't even ask.

Earl carries a stack of foam take-out containers. Zenia enters from the kitchen, bag in hand, ready to depart.

EARL

She takin' her nap?

ZENIA

Um-hmm . . .
              (eyes Thomas)
But she needs a bath.

LORETTA
              (exits, muttering)
Tell you one thing . . . Labor Day can't get here fast
enough for me. . . .

Exiting, Zenia's smile and voice are less even than usual:

ZENIA

She sure got that right. . . .

EARL
              (to Thomas)
What you lookin' at?

Thomas displays a photo album.

THOMAS

Pictures.

EARL

That's my son's family.
              (pointing)
That's your cousin, Will, he's a lawyer . . . and his wife,
Monica. . . . the two boys are Collin, he's fourteen . . .
and Justin, he's ten.

THOMAS
              (half-heartedly)
They live 'round here?

EARL

>They're in Atlanta, but you'll get to meet 'em. . . .
>They're all comin' over for Annie's birthday next
>month.

Earl walks away. Thomas glumly stares down at the picture.

WHAT HE SEES: Smiling faces, a Christmas tree, and all the toys, games, electronic gear and sports equipment that affluent parents could possibly lavish onto their kids.

EXT. COUNTRYSIDE — DUSK

The last blush of daylight fades beyond the treeline.

EXT. FRONT PORCH — DUSK

Loretta paces, restlessly surveying the vastly empty landscape. She gamely sits in a porch rocker and awkwardly tries a few rocks. Immediately bored, she gets up and walks toward the door.

INT. KITCHEN — DUSK

Annie watches Earl plop a chicken fillet into a food processor.

EARL

>OK, we gonna try out a new recipe here. The first thing
>we gotta do is grind up the chicken.
>>*(finger on the button)*
>You ready?

Her staring eyes gleam. Earl smiles and turns on the blender.

INT. LIVING ROOM — DUSK

Thomas and Tracy are on the floor with the Tiger. Tracy is in her "emotionless automaton" mode, and Thomas tries to engage her by bobbing the tiger's head in speech.

THOMAS

An' when we get back to Chicago, we gonna be makin'
money again, an' we gonna get big an' fat . . .
(offers her the tiger)
You wanna do it for a while?

INT. KITCHEN—DUSK

*Earl and Annie dubiously stare at the goop in the blender. Loretta enters, looks,
and gags.*

LORETTA

What *is* that?

EARL

Horseradish cilantro creamed chicken . . . What you
think?

LORETTA
(flat revulsion)
I'm just tellin' you *right now*, I ain't never gonna dip my
fingers to even *touch* that stuff!
(Earl chuckles)
You oughtta shut that place down and open you up a
Pop-Eye's. . . .

EARL
(to Annie)
Baby, would you please get me a lemon from the
'frigerator?

Annie shuffles over to the refrigerator and opens the door.

LORETTA

Is there a taxi or somethin' that can take me to town?

EARL

What for? Nothin' open there anyway.

LORETTA
(considers)
How far away is Jackson?

EARL
About a hundred dollars. Each way.

Annie returns with an egg, not a lemon. Earl takes it.

EARL
Thank you, baby.

LORETTA
(turns)
I'll get you a lemon.

EARL
(reflexively)
No, no, no.
(catches himself)
It's OK, she knows *exactly* what she's doin'.

He cracks the egg, pours it in the bowl and smiles at Annie.

EARL
She knows *exactly* what she's doin'.

INT. LIVING ROOM—DUSK

Loretta wanders in to find Thomas bobbing the tiger's head.

THOMAS
An' we gonna give Gramma Rosa a great big hug. . . .

*Loretta joins them on the floor, takes the tiger from Thomas and makes it add
her own thoughts:*

An' we gonna have us some *real* food, and drink us a
great big ol' beer. . . .

Thomas tensely watches Loretta squeeze the stuffed tiger.

INT. KITCHEN—MORNING

*They're at the breakfast table, Earl in a suit; Thomas in nice trousers and a tie
that's way too big for him; Annie in quite possibly every piece of jewelry she owns.
Tracy's in a frilly pink outfit, and Thomas works hard to keep her away from
the food. Annie's impatient.*

ANNIE

Can we go?

EARL

Right after we finish eatin' our breakfast.

Loretta shuffles in, bleary-eyed and in her robe.

EARL

I guess you decided not to go to church with us after
all.

LORETTA
(pours coffee)
I could use some quiet time to myself.

EARL

You gonna miss a good time. We're goin' up to
Clarksdale after, for a good Sunday dinner.
(a beat)
To a place that's got more'n just chicken. . . .

THOMAS
(To Tracy, annoyed)
Now why you do that?

Tracy gleefully smears jelly all over herself. Earl shakes his head and watches Loretta from the corner of his eye.

> EARL
>
> Oh, that's too bad. I guess she'll just have to stay home with you, Loretta.
>
> *(a beat)*
>
> I'm sure the two of you'll have a real nice, quiet time together. . . .

EXT. COUNTRY CHURCH — DAY

Small and simple, and could use a fresh coat of paint. Cars are parked in the gravel out front.

INT. CHURCH SANCTUARY — DAY

The preaching REVEREND FLOYD seems older than dust.

> REV. FLOYD
>
> . . . So even though we believe in the Lord to make miracles . . .

> MAN IN CONGREGATION
>
> Yes, we do . . .

The ELDERLY CONGREGATION fan themselves and punctuate the minister's words with random amens *and other comments.*

> REV. FLOYD
>
> They don't always come in the way that we expect. . . .

> MAN IN CONGREGATION
>
> No, they don't. . . .

Near the front, Earl listens as Annie mumbles and stares at the watches on her wrist. Thomas discreetly looks around.

REV. FLOYD

So we *pray* for the Lord to work His miracle in *others*, if
He so desires. . . .

Loretta, bored, restrains a cleaned-up Tracy on her lap.

REV. FLOYD

But if He doesn't . . .

ANNIE
(annoyed)

What time is it?

REV. FLOYD
(wary eyes on Annie)

Then we pray for Him to work His miracle in *us*.

EARL

Sshh . . . It's almost time to sing.

ANNIE
(much too loudly)

I want to sing *now*.

REV. FLOYD
(abruptly)

Let's open our songbooks to page forty-two, and show
the Lord how much we *believe* in miracles!

Loretta snickers. Others smile as they stand. The organ pipes up, and Earl hands Loretta an open hymnal.

Earl and Annie join in, but what Annie's mouthing is not the hymn. Tracy watches her. Thomas gamely tries to participate. Loretta stays silent.

Now Tracy emits a low wail, much like a hound baying along with the music. Loretta immediately looks down at the hymnal and sings over Tracy's sounds. People grin and chuckle. One GRINNING MAN nudges his DOZING WIFE, who wakens with a start.

As Tracy pumps up the volume, so does Loretta, until they belt it out like the choir swaying up front. The place is energized, with everyone but Loretta enjoying themselves enormously.

EXT. CHURCH STOOP — DAY

After the service, people file out past Reverend Floyd.

> DOZING WOMAN
> That was a wonderful sermon, Reverend Floyd.

> REV. FLOYD
> Thank you, Miz Smalls.

> GRINNING MAN
> Short. To the point. I like that.
> *(cackles to Earl)*
> You know, you oughtta bring them to church more often!

Reverend Floyd eyes Earl's group with genuine pleasure.

> REV. FLOYD
> It sure is good to see young people in the church again.
> *(to Loretta)*
> You got a good, strong voice, Sister. We could use a voice like that in the choir.

LORETTA
(politely aloof)

We only gonna be here a few weeks.

REV. FLOYD

Well, you give it some thought.

Loretta continues down the steps.

EARL
(raising his eyebrows)

Her mother turned Jehovah's.

Reverend Floyd nods "Ahhh" with wise understanding.

EXT. CHURCH CEMETERY—DAY

Earl gives them a tour of the small, tidy cemetery.

THOMAS
(surveying headstones)

A whole lotta Sinclairs.

EARL

Five generations' worth.
(points)
That's my mama and daddy.

The twin headstones indicate that George Sinclair died in 1941; Clara in 1972.

EARL

They were your great-grandparents.
(another point)
That's Jesse.

Those dates read 1847–1922. The adjacent headstone for Lucy Sinclair reads 1850–1920.

THOMAS

Nathan's Jesse?

EARL

Uh-huh. He helped start the church, over a hundred
years ago.

THOMAS
(ponders)

That's a long time.

EARL

Not so long . . .
(appraises Thomas)
Can you picture it?

THOMAS
(shakes his head)

Not really.

*Earl sits on a tree stump almost six feet in diameter, and indicates for Thomas
to do the same.*

EARL

See this tree stump?
(off Thomas's nod)
This oak tree was real old when it died a few years ago.
It was already full grown in Jesse's time. When he was
a boy, he used to sit under its shade. See them rings?
Ev'ry ring is a year in a tree's life, and ev'ry one of 'em
tells a little story.

He picks up some pebbles and places one on the stump.

EARL

This ring remembers the year eighteen fifty-four, when
the white Sinclairs came over from Alabama, and
brought Jesse with 'em.
(Thomas intently watches Earl place more pebbles)

EARL

And this one's eighteen sixty-five, when the Civil War
ended, and Jesse was given his freedom. This one's
eighteen seventy-two, when Jesse started the church,
right next to the shade of his favorite tree.

*Loretta also listens. Behind her, Annie and Tracy pull at some weeds. Earl places
another pebble.*

EARL

This one's nineteen fifty-one, when I went off to the
Korean War, and your grandparents moved to Chicago.

THOMAS
(surveys the rings)

Where was I born?

EARL

When were you born? Nineteen eighty-five?
(off Thomas's nod)
The tree died back in 'eighty, and we had to cut it
down.

Off Thomas's disappointment, he points out a younger tree.

EARL

But you see that tree over there? I happened to plant
that tree the very same year you were born. Now, you
and my son Will can pass along the family history to
your own kids someday.

*Thomas appears relieved; Loretta, impressed. Annie appears and presents Earl
with a clump of weeds.*

EARL
(touched)

Why, thank you, baby. These are right pretty.

EXT. CHURCH PARKING LOT—DAY

They stroll toward the car, Earl holding the weeds in one hand, Annie's hand in the other.

> EARL
>
> What you gonna do with yourself when you're all grown up?

> THOMAS
>
> Dunno if I'll make it that far.

> EARL
>
> Oh, yes you will, I promise. Your grandmother'll make sure of that.

> THOMAS
>
> I just wanna get me and Tracy and Gramma Rosa as far away from the projects as we can get.
> *(off Loretta's nudge)*
> Oh yeah, and Mama, too.

INT. LIVING ROOM—EVENING

Loretta's on the phone, with an antsy Thomas nearby. She rolls her eyes as intense sounds stream from the receiver.

> LORETTA
>
> Uh-huh . . . Uh-huh . . . Uh-huh . . .

She just hands it to Thomas and walks away. It takes him a few moments to break in.

> THOMAS
>
> Gramma Rosa? . . . Yes ma'am, it's me. . . . Uh-huh . . .
> It's OK . . . Lookin' after Tracy . . .

INTERCUT WITH:

INT. ROSA LYNN'S LIVING ROOM—EVENING

> ROSA LYNN
> *(rocking in her chair)*
> Now, what you need to do is get outta that big ol' house
> and just enjoy bein' a child. . . . That's right. First thing
> in the mornin', you ought to go right out in the middle
> of one of those great, big fields and run 'round and yell,
> just like a wild, crazy fool. . . .

INT. EARL'S LIVING ROOM—EVENING

Thomas chuckles off her suggestion.

> THOMAS
> Yes, ma'am. . . . Uh-huh, I promise. . . . OK . . .
> *(lowers the receiver)*
> Mama, she say you get back here right now! . . . She
> ain't done with you yet!

We BEGIN A MONTAGE, where everybody settles into the summer:

EXT. CATFISH POND—DAY

*Earl, in hip-waders, tries to coax a similarly clad Thomas—they're chest-waders
on him—into joining him in the water. But no way Thomas is going in there.*

INT. LIVING ROOM—DAY

*Tracy stands atop the coffee table, with arms stretched out from her sides and
solemn eyes dead ahead. She stiffly holds that position and falls, face forward,
right onto the floor.*

Now we reveal Annie, applauding wildly from the couch.

INT. JUST CHICKEN — DAY

The serving room is packed, with Gina and Isabelle running hard and Earl busily working the register.

INT. JUST CHICKEN KITCHEN — DAY

The cook gracefully juggles pans over burners. Loretta stuffs sausages just as fast as she can.

EXT. HUGE OPEN FIELD — DAY

Thomas "walks" Tracy on her leash. He releases her, and takes delight in seeing her scamper about in the open space.

His smile fades when she runs off in a hard beeline for the middle of the field. He takes off after her, runnin' and yellin' in the middle of the field, just like his Gramma Rosa suggested.

EXT. EARL'S FRONT YARD — MAGIC HOUR

Our MONTAGE CONCLUDES: Earl helps Thomas replace the seat of the broken tree swing. Loretta holds Tracy on her lap to take the inaugural ride.

INT. JUST CHICKEN — DAY

The end of the workday, and Earl hands Loretta her paycheck. When she looks at it, she's not impressed.

> **LORETTA**
> This don't seem like much money for stuffin' a million sausages.
> *(looks up)*
> How 'bout payin' me by the link?

Earl just smiles. Loretta looks over to where Gina and Isabelle sit at a table and count their tips.

LORETTA

Then how 'bout lettin' me waitress, so I can make some
tip money?

EARL
(considers)

We can do that. . . .
(she brightens)
But I still need you to make the sausages. You mind
comin' in early 'nough to get that job done before we
open up?

LORETTA
(disappointed)

I'll think about it.

INT. LIVING ROOM — DAY

Earl and Loretta arrive home from work. Passing Thomas and Tracy in the
living room, Loretta rhythmically harangues Earl:

LORETTA

Fried chicken, grilled chicken, boiled chicken, baked
chicken! . . .

THOMAS
(teasing)

Hey, Mama. What's for dinner?

LORETTA
(glares, continues)
. . . Chicken stew, chicken hash, chicken on a stick! . . .
Isn't there some other food on this earth that don't
cluck when you eat it?!

As Earl exits toward the kitchen with his foam take-out containers, she calls
after:

LORETTA

You ever hear of hamburgers made with *real* meat?!

THOMAS
(*without enthusiasm*)
What he bring home this time?

LORETTA

Those tarragon chicken burgers again.

Thomas whimpers and buries his face in his hands. Zenia has entered to overhear this. She first smiles, then sympathetically eyes Thomas.

ZENIA

Why don't you two come home with me for supper?

THOMAS
(*immediately brightens*)
Can we, Mama?

Loretta warily eyes Zenia, whose smile looks extra "spacey."

LORETTA

What're we gonna eat?

ZENIA

We got pork chops, steak, real hamburgers . . . as much red meat as you want.

THOMAS

Real hamburgers, Mama? *Please?*

INT. ZENIA'S TOYOTA—DAY

Thomas listens in from the back.

LORETTA

How long you been lookin' after Annie?

ZENIA

I've been going out to the house full-time about, oh, three years now.

LORETTA

How do you do it? Don't it make you a little crazy?
(*backpedals*)
I mean, at first, I wondered what kindsa drugs you were doin', always bein' so patient and all.

Off Thomas's muffled snicker, Loretta briefly looks pissed.

ZENIA

I'm not always like this, it just takes me a while to get back to normal. But after a while you figure out that sometimes its just easier to *join* the madness instead of fightin' it. That makes it easy to find ways to deal with her.

LORETTA

How's that . . . ?

ZENIA

Well, like when she's *really* gettin' on your nerves, just ask her to go to the 'frigerator and fetch somethin' impossible, like a red grapefruit. . . .
(*low chuckle*)
Now, *that* one's good for an hour of peace and quiet. . . .

Loretta appraises Zenia with a new appreciation.

EXT. ZENIA'S HOUSE—DAY

They get out of the car in front of a cluster of five rather new, but small and simple brick houses.

LORETTA

They look new.

ZENIA

They *are* new. Three years ago, Earl helped us buy the
land and got Habitat for Humanity to come in and build
the houses.
(*eyes one with pride*)
It's not much, but it's all mine. I even helped build it.

INT. ZENIA'S LIVING ROOM—DAY

*Entering through the screen door, Zenia sees the living room in disarray and
immediately bellows at the top of her lungs:*

ZENIA

Cassandra! Terrence! Get your butts out here!

*Fifteen-year-old CASSANDRA and 10-year-old TERRENCE immediately
appear and frantically start tidying up.*

ZENIA
(*braying drill seargent*)
What *is* this?! Don't you *know* I work hard all day,
keepin' somebody else's house?! I don't *even* need to
come home to find my own lookin' like some kinda
trash dump!

Loretta gapes at the New Zenia, who abruptly turns to her:

ZENIA

You want a beer?

EXT. ZENIA'S FRONT STOOP—EVENING

Later. Loretta and Zenia sit on the stoop with their beers.

ZENIA

Leon's not a bad guy. He gives money when he can and
comes up to see the kids most ev'ry weekend.

LORETTA

At least he's still in the picture. Mine took off after
Tracy was born. Just couldn't handle it. That's when
we moved in with my mother.

ZENIA

That can't be too easy. . . .

LORETTA
(drinks deep)

No. It most certainly is not.

The kids appear on the other side of the screen door.

CASSANDRA

We all done with the dishes, Mom. Can we watch TV
now?

ZENIA

Yes, you can.
(calls after)
You let Thomas choose the show, now.

Loretta's eyes wistfully linger beyond the screen door.

LORETTA

Two healthy kids . . .

Zenia stares down at her beer.

LORETTA

Lemme ask you something . . . When you look at Tracy,
what do you see?

ZENIA
(awkwardly)

Well . . .

(matter of factly)

Well, I thought maybe she was a crack baby. Or
something like that.

LORETTA
(earnestly)

No, that's OK. That's just you, and the rest of the
world. But she's autistic.

ZENIA

Does that mean she's always gonna be like that?

LORETTA
(looks away)

Yeah, basically. And there's nothin' I can do about it. I
look at your daughter, and I try to picture what Tracy's
gonna be like at her age . . . but . . .

(shakes her head)

I can't even . . .

ZENIA

Lemme ask you something. . . . When Tracy looks at
you, what do you think she sees?

(matter of factly)

Her Mama. She sees *you*, her Mama.

Loretta ponders this. Zenia shrugs and drinks her beer.

INT. EARL'S ENTRY HALL—NIGHT

As a drained Loretta locks the front door, she and Thomas overhear Earl, apparently on the telephone:

> EARL (OS)
>
> You *have* to come, Will, it's her birthday. . . .

INT. LIVING ROOM—NIGHT

Earl is on the phone, perched on the edge of his chair.

> EARL
>
> She's only gonna be with us a few more years, Will, and we have to make the most of every year we can.
> *(listens)*
> You're wrong, you're flat wrong. . . . She's still your mother and she still knows who you are. . . .

INT. FRONT HALL—NIGHT

Loretta and Thomas quietly start up the stairs.

> EARL (OS)
>
> What do you mean, "space"? We got plenty of space for ev'rybody, the boys'll have fun campin' out together in the livin' room.

> LORETTA
> *(whispers to Thomas)*
> You go on up to bed.

> EARL (OS)
>
> They're family too, Will.

Loretta's expression hardens a bit.

EXT. FRONT PORCH — DAY

The entire family's out on the front porch as a car pulls into the drive. Earl smiles and starts down the steps.

> EARL
>
> There they are.
> > *(looks back)*
> You comin'?

> LORETTA
> > *(evenly)*
> We'll wait up here with Annie.

Earl greets the family tumbling out of the late-model Volvo.

> EARL
>
> Right on time!

Mid-30s WILL and MONICA look pure suburban. Their sons argue over a soccer ball—fourteen-year-old COLLIN holding it just out of reach above ten-year-old JUSTIN'S head.

JUSTIN

You said I could have it when we got here!

COLLIN

(teasing-big-brother tone)

Not till you ask me real nice . . .

JUSTIN

D-a-a-d! . . .

Loretta surveys the scene without enthusiasm.

LORETTA

Well . . . at least the car's black.

Thomas takes uneasy note of her attitude.

MINUTES LATER

Everybody's a little on edge as the introductions are made.

EARL

This is Loretta, Thomas, and Tracy.

The adults exchange awkward hellos. Monica sees Tracy, smiles with delight and moves closer.

MONICA

Isn't she just adorable? . . .

Loretta sees Tracy's eyes narrow, and grabs Monica's arm before it's too late.

LORETTA

Don't you get too close to her.

Monica gives Loretta a look. Will crouches before Annie.

WILL

Hello, Mama.

(no response)

It's me, Mama . . . Will, your son.

Annie tenses and stares blankly. She relaxes when Loretta pats her on the shoulder.

LORETTA

It's OK . . . We're right here.

Will tries to read Loretta's impassive expression.

INT. DINING ROOM—NIGHT

Everybody's packed around the table. Annie and Tracy finger-feed each other. With conversation faltering, Earl motions to Loretta, so she directs a question to Collin:

LORETTA

So . . . you still in school?

Off the silence, Loretta looks around. Maybe too patiently:

MONICA

Collin and Justin go to a special school, one that
teaches all the students in a foreign language.

WILL
(prompts Collin)
Go on, say something in Spanish.

ERIC
(slyly eyes Thomas)
Estas disfrutando el verano, Thomas?

THOMAS
(eyes narrow)
What you mean by that?

Collin snickers, then catches his father's warning glance.

ERIC

I was just asking if you were having a good summer.

THOMAS
(muttering)

I *was* . . .

LORETTA
(to Justin)
You know Spanish, too?

JUSTIN

Ahreeko wah-nah, ohreegah-mee, ghee-ro masuki . . .
Waka rheema senji-su?

Loretta and Thomas stare. Justin dissolves into giggles.

MONICA

Well, with the Japanese becoming such a world
economic power and all, it just made sense . . .

EXT. FRONT PORCH — NIGHT

Will and Earl sit alone, slowly rocking.

> **WILL**
>
> How can she see me as her son, when she thinks
> somebody else is her own dead mother?

> **EARL**
>
> If she saw more of you, some things would come back.

> **WILL**
>
> Dad, we've been over this a hundred times. I'm *not*
> gonna move my family to Mississippi. We've got our
> own lives in Atlanta.

> **EARL**
>
> But your roots are here.

Will stands and walks towards the door, with Earl following.

INT. LIVING ROOM — NIGHT

Everyone but Annie is bored with I Love Lucy *on TV. Tracy sleeps and drools on Annie's lap. Will enters, followed by Earl.*

> **WILL**
>
> You boys got enough sheets and pillows?

> **LORETTA**
> (*stands*)
>
> Thomas is gonna sleep with us tonight.
> (*picks up Tracy*)
> Give ev'rybody their "space."

INT. KITCHEN — EARLY MORNING

Loretta enters the quiet, empty kitchen and automatically reaches for the Maxwell House can. Finding a pot already brewed, she glances around and instead reaches for a mug.

EXT. FRONT PORCH—EARLY MORNING

Loretta comes out the front door. Seeing Will perched on the tree swing with his coffee, she considers going back inside, but instead steps down from the porch.

EXT. FRONT YARD—EARLY MORNING

Loretta approaches Will with her coffee.

> LORETTA
>
> Good mornin'. . . .

> WILL
>
> Mornin'. Always up this early on a Sunday?

> LORETTA
> *(a little surprised by her own answer)*
> Yeah, guess so . . . lately.

> WILL
>
> Last time I sat in this swing was maybe . . . thirty pounds ago or something.

> LORETTA
>
> Musta been broken for a while. Your father fixed it up for the kids.

> WILL
>
> Hmmm . . . never did that for my kids. Not that they'd use it, anyway. Not when they got their computer games and fifty channels of cable TV to choose from.

> LORETTA
>
> Too bad you live so far away. I know he wishes he could see more of them.

                          WILL

And I wish I didn't have to bill sixty hours a week just
to keep even.
                      (more to himself)
You can work so hard to get where you want to be. . . .
And then, when you get there . . .

He's lost in thought for a beat, then looks to Loretta.

                       LORETTA

You askin' *me?*

                          WILL
                      (sheepishly)
Yeah, I guess not. . . .

Realizing the awkward turn in conversation, he stands.

                          WILL

Well, whatever, you know what I mean.
                      (sheepish exit)
I'm . . . gonna go get some more coffee now. . . .

                       LORETTA
                      (dry smile)
Good idea.

Loretta's sympathetic eyes stay on his departing back.

                       LORETTA

Mm-mm-mmm . . .

EXT. BACK PATIO — AFTERNOON

*The four kids kick around the soccer ball in the distant background. Seated at
the picnic table, Monica watches Earl stoke the coals in the grill.*

EARL

I know it's hard on him. I know every time he sees her
it's like seeing it all over again for the very first time.

MONICA

Maybe he sees himself.
                    (off Earl's quizzical look)
I think he worries about it being . . . not catching, but
hereditary or something.

EARL

He thinks a man his age got to worry 'bout
Alzheimer's?

MONICA

Every time he forgets something, he gets this . . . look.

EARL

Well, I can fix *that*.

MONICA

No, please don't say anything. That would only make
things . . . harder.

EARL

                    (ponders a beat)
You two doing better these days?

MONICA

                    (shrugs)
Working at it harder, anyway.

INT. KITCHEN—DAY

*Loretta prepares coleslaw. Annie—in her "birthday girl" party hat—tries to
"help" Will ice the cake.*

WILL

Technically, it's big-time corporate law . . . but in my practice, I use it on a smaller, more entrepreneurial basis.

Annie reaches for Will's knife.

ANNIE

I want to do it.
                    (growing petulant)
I *always* do it.

LORETTA

Aunt Annie, would you do me a favor?
                    (Annie looks at her)
Would you please go fetch me a red grapefruit from the 'frigerator?

Puzzled, Will watches Annie shuffle towards the refrigerator.

WILL

A *red* grapefruit . . . ?

LORETTA

Don't fight her. Join her.
                    (back to conversation)
What's . . .
                    (stumbles on the word)
. . . "entrepreneurial"?

WILL

It's hard to explain. . . .
                    (a bit patronizing)
Well, it's about how to help the economically disenfranchised to rise above their surroundings by starting little business enterprises of their own.
                    (gets into it)
You start by finding out what new products people *really* want, then you figure out how to sell it to them.

He's thrown by Loretta's earnest and emphatic nod:

> LORETTA
>
> Oh, I know all 'bout *that*.

EXT. BACKYARD — DAY

The kids kick the ball around, Eric letting Thomas play as little as possible. Tracy happily chases after it.

INT. KITCHEN — DAY

Annie mumbles into the open refrigerator. Loretta has apparently scored a breakthrough of some kind:

> WILL
>
> You got it, that's it *exactly* . . . You start small, one customer at a time, but before you know it, you've built a *huge* base of loyal customers, one by one. Eventually, you'll need to hire more people to manage the business. It's a *never*-ending process of expansion, an *endless* cycle of growth!
>   *(swirls icing with passion)*
> And *that* is what I'm talking about! *Jobs*, Loretta! Jobs for the community!

Recovering, he licks icing from the knife.

> WILL
>
> Tell me something . . . What exactly does this "Marco" sell, anyway?

Loretta's mischievous smile broadens to "gotcha."

EXT. BACK PATIO — DAY

Earl and Monica are still at the grill.

EARL

I'm telling you, life out here is quiet 'nough to give you two the time you need to remember why you got together in the first place.

MONICA

(patient sigh)

I'm sure . . .

EARL

Marianna's not all that different from Atlanta anyway. Always room for one more lawyer.

Monica is relieved to see Will come out of the house with a bowl of food. He places it on the table with the look of a martyr.

MONICA

How are you doing in there?

WILL

(glances at the house)

I guess I'll make it.

Off Monica's small smile, Earl's own expression sours a bit.

EXT. SIDE YARD—DAY

Disgusted with being toyed with, Thomas turns to walk away.

> **THOMAS**
> C'mon, Tracy. Let's go see what Mama's doin'.

Collin kicks the ball into some bushes, and Tracy scurries after it. Thomas moves to follow.

> **THOMAS**
> Don't you go in there. . . .
> > *(crouches)*
>
> C'mon, Tracy.
> > *(pries apart brush)*
>
> Tracy . . . ?

She emerges, squealing and clutching something small that she thrusts right at his face. Thomas freezes.

EXT. BACK PATIO—DAY

> **THOMAS (OS)**
> SNAKE!! . . . SNAKE!!

Earl, Will and Monica start running.

INT. KITCHEN—DAY

> **LORETTA**
> > *(looks out the window)*
>
> Omigod! . . .
> > *(runs out the door)*
>
> Thomas?! . . . Tracy?!

EXT. BACKYARD — DAY

Thomas trembles at the remains of a very small and dead snake dangling from Tracy's hand. Suppressing a smile, Earl takes it from her and tosses it.

> ### EARL
> It's just a garden snake. A harmless little garden snake, and it's dead. It can't hurt anybody.

Loretta arrives in time to hear this.

> ### LORETTA
> You OK, Thomas?

As Thomas shakes off his mother to recover his age-twelve manhood, he sees Collin's struggle to contain laughter.

> ### COLLIN
> Nada más era una culebra, stupido?

Humiliated, Thomas charges with a fury, his lowered head barreling right into the "Oomph!!" of Collin's soft belly.

INT. KITCHEN — DAY

Annie turns from the refrigerator to smile at the open door.

EXT. SIDE YARD — DAY

Will pulls the two scuffling boys apart.

> ### WILL
> You boys cut it out!
> *(to Thomas)*
> You keep your hands to yourself, you understand?!
> Save that kinda stuff for back where you come from.

LORETTA

Hey! Nobody speaks to my kid like that but *me*, you
hear me?!

Will and Monica herd their boys away. To Will:

MONICA

You see what I mean? *This* is what I've been talking
about! We just don't belong here!

LORETTA
(fierce sputters)

Uh-huh, that's right, that's right. . . . You just take
yourselves and go back to your fancy house in Atlanta!
Just stay away from me and my family!

Earl suddenly passes her, heading fast for the house.

EXT. BACK PATIO—DAY

*Annie's heaped at the bottom of the steps, struggling to get up. Earl runs up and
crouches beside her.*

EARL

You OK, baby?

(*lightly restrains her*)

No, no. No, no, no.

(*tests her limbs*)

Lemme just look at you for a minute.

WILL

(*arrives scared*)

She OK?

Annie struggles with Earl, who sighs with relief.

EARL

Yeah, she's OK.

(*helps her up*)

OK, real slow, now. R-e-e-e-a-l slow . . .

Annie seems buoyed by her adventure. Everybody eyes Earl and Loretta uneasily.

WILL

Come on, let's get inside.

(*Collin smiles*)

Right now, Collin.

Will's family goes inside. Aware of Annie, Earl smiles and keeps his tone pleasant, but his words are tinged with fury. The combination is a bit schizophrenic.

EARL

You wanna destroy your family? *Fine*, can't do nothin' about that. But you will *not* stay here and destroy mine, you understand?

Loretta stares back helplessly, then defiantly.

THOMAS

C'mon, Mama . . . Mama? . . .

She takes Thomas by the arm and, carrying Tracy, leads him up the steps and into the house. Annie looks brightly at Earl.

> ANNIE
> Where's my cake?

EXT. EARL'S HOUSE—DAY

Later that day. Will's family is in their car. Earl leans against Will's open window.

> EARL
> You still comin' over Labor Day?

> WILL
> (glances at the house)
> They be gone by then?

Off Collin's muffled snicker, Earl registers disappoinent.

> EARL
> Yeah.

Will starts the car.

INT. LORETTA'S BEDROOM—DAY

Loretta discreetly observes Earl watch the car turn onto the road. When he turns and looks up, she steps from the window.

LATER, SAME LOCATION

Thomas stands in the doorway, glumly looking inside.

WHAT HE SEES: Loretta's seated on the far side of the bed with her back to us, her head bowed.

Thomas quietly walks away. Now the camera reveals that Loretta is staring down at the pawn ticket she's fingering.

INT. EARL'S LIVING ROOM—DAY

Earl stares moodily at the Polaroid of Rosa Lynn and Nathan on the fireplace mantel. A low rumble signals that storm clouds are gathering.

INT. LORETTA'S BEDROOM—NIGHT

The dark is broken by a lightning flash, with a hard rain falling. Loretta wakes with a start, turns on the lamp, and looks over at Tracy asleep in her crib. Along with the thunder, Loretta hears an argument coming from downstairs.

INT. FRONT HALLWAY—NIGHT

As Loretta creeps down the stairs, the sounds become clearer—it sounds like Annie's having some kind of fit.

> ANNIE (OS)
> *(garbled hysteria)*
> Why are you just *standin'* there?! *Do* something!

> EARL (OS)
> *(soothing, helpless)*
> What do you want me to do, Annie? Just tell me what you want, and I'll do it!

INT. LIVING ROOM—NIGHT

When Loretta peeks into the living room, her eyes pop.

WHAT SHE SEES: Annie rushes from window to window like a wild animal, her face contorted and long nightgown flapping.

> ANNIE
> *(garbled terror)*
> We gotta *do* somethin'! . . . We can't just leave 'em there, they'll be washed away!

Earl follows, trying to calm and protect her.

EARL

Slow down, baby, just slow down. You runnin' around
isn't gonna help anybody.

Earl notices Loretta and motions for her to come over. Loretta's paralyzed, so he
crosses to her.

EARL

Just go straight into the kitchen and call Zenia. Tell her
to call back here right away, then you hang up. When
the phone rings, let me answer it.
                    (she hesitates)
Go on! Don't worry 'bout wakin' Zenia, she'll
understand.

Loretta exits. Earl returns to Annie, who's wailing, her face pressed aginst the
window. Off sudden lightning, she jumps back, screaming, arms flailing.

EARL

We gotta let the sheriff take care of it, Annie. He knows
what he's doin' . . .

ANNIE

Maybe he can't get to them! Maybe it's too late!

As the phone rings, she presses her face against the window.

EARL

You hear that? It's the phone, Annie.
                    (rings continue)
Answer the phone, baby. Maybe it's the sheriff, with
some good news.
                    (loudly answers)
Hello . . . ?
                    (exaggerated relief)
Hello Sheriff Odom . . .
                    (brightens)
You did? You got 'em all out? Every single last one of
'em . . . ?

Loretta watches with morbid fascination from the entry hall.

EARL

You hear that, Annie? Sheriff Odom says he done
rescued all of 'em!
(eyes Annie's back)
Uh-huh, ev'rybody got rescued from the flood . . . Uh-
huh, ev'rybody got rescued from the flood. . . .
(Annie's calming)
You hear that, baby? Sheriff Odom says that ev'rybody
got rescued from the flood. . . .

Annie snuffles at the window, her back to us and Earl.

EARL

Just in time, Annie . . . He got out every single last one,
just in time . . .

*Annie slowly turns to face us squarely, to reveal that a bridge of her teeth is
missing. Earl motions for her.*

EARL

Thank you, Sheriff Odom. Thank you ever so much.

*Annie slowly walks towards Earl, crying softly, her energy spent. Earl hangs up
and tenderly puts his arms around her.*

EARL

It's OK . . . It's OK . . .
(eases for the couch)
Sheriff Odom got out ev'rybody, each and ev'ry one of
'em.
(sits down with her)
And he says he's gonna bring 'em all by for a visit, first
thing in the mornin'. . . .

*Mouthing thank you, Earl motions to Loretta to go back to bed. She numbly
turns away. He gently rocks Annie.*

EARL

Now, won't that be nice? Why, we haven't seen them
in such a long, long time. . . .

EXT. SURROUNDING COUNTRYSIDE — MORNING

Last night's storm has washed everything clean.

INT. KITCHEN — MORNING

Sipping coffee at the table, Earl appears as if nothing had happened the night before. Loretta enters, pours herself a cup and joins him at the table.

> LORETTA
>
> How's Aunt Annie doin'?

> EARL
>
> Just fine, sleepin' like a little baby.
> *(off her expression)*
> Really nothin' to worry about. When she wakes up, it'll be like last night never even happened.

> LORETTA
>
> She get that way much?

> EARL
>
> Every once in a while, maybe a coupla times a year. In a strange way, I kinda like it when she does. It means she's still fightin' it, a part of her's still right here with me.
> *(almost beams)*
> Did you *hear* her last night? She was makin' real sentences!

Loretta indicates that well, yeah, she was doing that.

> EARL
>
> You know, sometimes she'll surprise you in other ways, too. One day, right outta the blue, she might just look you right in the eye and say, clear as a bell, "Who are you, and why are you in my house?"

Silence, as Loretta avoids his eyes. Finally:

LORETTA

If, um, that ever happens . . . What should I say?

EARL
(eyes twinkle)

Well, it would prob'ly confuse her to hear exactly who
you are. Just tell her you're a friend of Zenia's, and
that'll make her very happy.
(turns serious)
You know . . . I know you haven't had it easy,
Loretta. . . .
(preempts her)
You had it hard in ways I don't know 'bout and in ways
I may never understand. And maybe you feel like
sometimes you have to say or do certain things to make
it a little easier for yourself. . . . That don't make you
any different than most people. . . . It just don't make
you any better.
(stands)
We better get ready for work. We got a whole lotta
chickens waitin'.

INT. LIVING ROOM—EVENING

*Earl, Loretta and Thomas watch TV. The lead news story is about a deranged
man entering a Shaker Heights post office and shooting everyone in range before
shooting himself.*

EARL

Will you look at that?
(shakes his head)
What's the world comin' to?

LORETTA
(dryly)

Uh-huh.

EARL

You don't think it's terrible?

LORETTA

Of course it's terrible. It's just that shootings like that
happen all the time back home. Nobody goes on TV
then to talk 'bout what a "tragedy" it is.

THOMAS

What kinda gun you think it was?

LORETTA

I dunno. Didn't they say it was a handgun?

THOMAS

Think so . . .
                    (considers)
Prob'ly a deuce-five.

Eyes widening, Earl uses the remote to lower the TV's volume.

LORETTA

Why you say that?

THOMAS
(ticks off his fingers)
Six shots. Small 'nough for your pocket. Get 'em
anyplace.

Earl leans forward a bit in his chair.

LORETTA

You don't think it was an automatic?

THOMAS

Nah, they say he shot real slow.
                    (mimics)
Pah! . . . Pah! . . . Pah!

Earl flinches with every Pah!

THOMAS
(*musing*)
Deuce-five. That be a good summer gun. . . .

EARL
(*baffled*)
What's a "summer gun"?

THOMAS
Small . . . You don't need a big coat to hide it. You
know, you can stick it under your shirt. . . .
(*demonstrates*)
Right here.

EARL
(*dumbfounded*)
How come you know so much about guns?

Loretta snickers.

THOMAS
Ev'rybody's got one back home.
(*wistfully*)
Well, ev'rybody but me, anyway.

EARL
Do you *want* one?!

THOMAS
Not 'xactly. But I sure will need one. When everybody
else is strapped, you gotta be strapped, too.

Loretta can't get over Earl's pitiful naiveté.

INT. JUST CHICKEN — DAY

*Loretta waitresses behind the counter. CARL, wearing a Southern Pride Poultry
workshirt, takes a counter stool and glumly squints up at the big, overhead
chalkboard menu.*

Hey, Carl, how you doin'?

CARL

Same ol', same ol' . . .

LORETTA

You don't look too happy today.

CARL

They talkin' about cuttin' back at the plant.
(dubious squint)
What the hell's "horseradish-cilantro creamed
chicken"?

LORETTA
(deadpan)
'Xactly what it sounds like.
(eyebrows shoot up)
On toast.

CARL

Think I'll stick with the fried dinner.

LORETTA

Good idea.

She approaches Earl at the register and hands him a checkpad.

LORETTA

I figure this one right?

Earl studies it, then picks up a pen to make a correction.

EARL

How you *really* feel about Thomas havin' a gun?

LORETTA

I'll put him off long as I can, but once he starts hangin'
around the older boys in school, there won't be a whole
lot I can do about it.

EARL

He in such a hurry to have a gun, then how come he's
still playin' around with that stuffed tiger?

LORETTA

I dunno, had it all his life. It basically keeps Tracy
company these days, though.

He starts to hand her the checkpad, but holds it back.

EARL

You mind if I buy Tracy a new one?

LORETTA
(shrugs)
Sure, why not? Ratty old thing's fallin' apart
anyway. . . .
(appraises Earl)
What you gettin' at? You lookin' like a man with a plan.

EARL

Wel-l-l-l . . . Seems like young Thomas needs a little
lesson in what guns are *really* 'bout.
(eyes twinkling)
Yes, I do believe it's time for ol' Mister Tiger to
retire. . . . And maybe even go out with a bang. . . .

He gives up the pad with a small, conspiratorial smile.

EXT. BACK FIELD — DAY

*Earl, Loretta and Thomas approach two "bulls-eye" targets propped atop
adjacent fence posts. Earl carries a double-barrel shotgun. Thomas is excited
enough to wet his pants.*

OK, about how far you reckon you'd be away from
someone, if you ever had to shoot?

THOMAS

I dunno.
(*guesses*)
Maybe 'bout . . . ten feet.

EARL

(*paces off ten feet*)
OK, this is pretty basic, but *important,* so you listen up.
(*demonstrates*)
Keep your feet apart to steady yourself.

Loretta stands a bit behind, nervously clutching her arms.

EARL

You got that?
(*Thomas nods*)
Brace the gun hard against your shoulder to steady it.
(*eye takes aim*)
Take your sweet time aimin', before you fire.

*As Earl raises the shotgun and takes aim, we're aware of its firm anchor against
his shoulder. When the gun goes off, Earl flinches from the kick and Loretta
from the noise. Thomas stares at the target in awe.*

THOMAS

Yo! Looka that! You done blowed it away!

*The mutilated target lies on the ground, next to the remains of a small grain
bag to which it was apparently attached.*

Earl hands him the rifle, and Thomas quietly gloats:

THOMAS

Yo, looka what I got, dudes . . . I got me a *shottie.* . . .

EARL
(seriously)

OK now, what's first?

THOMAS

Feets apart . . .

(does so)

Steady it . . .

(does so)

EARL

Brace it real firm, now.

(Thomas braces)

Now take your time aimin' . . .

Earl looks at Loretta and raises his eyebrows, and she nods weakly. He winks, which she returns with a weaker smile.

Breathing hard, Thomas begins a growl that grows into a roar:

THOMAS

ARRGGGHHHH!!

. . . and fires, the kick sending him into a near back flip. He scrambles up, whooping:

THOMAS

Yow! Did you see that?! Did you see that?! Man, I did
him! I did him *good*!

*He clutches his shoulder, but his grin is ear to ear. His euphoria is cut short
when he sees the target's remains.*

*WHAT HE SEES: Next to his target is not a grain bag, but the mutilated tiger,
surrounded by still drifting bits of green.*

EARL

Now, lemme tell you somethin' about what guns can do
to people. . . .

*His little speech is preempted by Thomas's howl, as he scrambles under the
barbed wire fence.*

THOMAS

Man! . . . What you do that for?!

LORETTA
(moves forward)

It's OK, Thomas, Uncle Earl's gonna buy Tracy a new
one. . . .
(sees the money)
What . . . ? Where'd that money come from?!

*Crying and bleeding, Thomas picks up the money and furiously tries to restuff
the shredded Tiger.*

LORETTA

You tell me!
(he ignores her)
Where'd you get that money?!

THOMAS
(faces her and screams)

It's *my* money, you understan', *mine*! I made it takin'
pictures of people downtown!

LORETTA

(softens)

What you thinkin' about, keepin' all that money stuffed
in the back of a toy tiger?

THOMAS

(sobbing)

'Cause I knew it'd be the one thing you'd never sell
away to get some drugs or liquor. . . .

Loretta is staggered by shame.

INT. KITCHEN — NIGHT

*Loretta and Thomas sit at the table and tape shredded bills back together.
Thomas's arms also look taped back together.*

LORETTA

When we get home, we gonna get you a savings
account, and nobody gonna touch that money but you.
Not me, not your Gramma Rosa, not Tracy, just you.

Observing him crookedly taping a bill, she reaches over.

LORETTA

Here, let's make it as perfect as your Gramma Rosa
would. . . .

(more to herself)

And after I find me a good job waitressin', we gonna
get another savings account, just for me.

THOMAS

Do we hafta go back? Can't we just stay here?

LORETTA

Yes, we have to go back. We have to think about your
Gramma Rosa, and what 'bout Nathan?

THOMAS
(like it's obvious)
Bring 'em down here.

LORETTA
We got to make our own home, Thomas.
(off his shrug, she puts one hand over his)
And I promise, it's gonna be a good one.

INT. JUST CHICKEN — DAY

*The end of the day, and Loretta's at the counter, pleased with counting her tips.
Earl empties the register.*

LORETTA
You know, maybe we should stay open for supper. If
people be willin' to come all the way from Yazoo City
for lunch, maybe they'll come up from Jackson for
supper.

EARL
I work hard 'nough as it is.

LORETTA
You ever thought about puttin' a big sign out on the
highway?
(Earl walks away)
Might bring in some truckers and tourists . . .
(brightens, calls after)
Hey, how 'bout a giant *movin'* sign, like the one we got
here?

INT. EARL'S KITCHEN — DAY

*Loretta and Thomas are again seated across from each other. In front of Loretta
is a filled cash drawer. Thomas eyes her, writes an amount on a check pad, then
hands it to her.*

LORETTA

That'll be three dollars and eighty-seven cents, please.

Thomas hands her a five dollar bill. Loretta contemplates the tray for only a moment, then scoops out change.

LORETTA

From five dollars . . . one dollar and thirteen cents's
your change.

THOMAS
(grins)

Yo . . . We lookin' good now.

He places the change down at his right, where Annie completes the process by sorting coins into various jars.

INT. LIVING ROOM—MORNING

Annie and Tracy have their eyes glued to Lucy on TV. Earl enters and pecks Annie on the cheek.

EARL

Bye-bye, Annie!

ANNIE
(absently, eyes on TV)

Bye-bye!

Earl shrugs, then heads for the front door. Loretta enters.

LORETTA

Bye-bye!

ANNIE
(eyes on TV)

Bye-bye!

Loretta absently pauses to fish in her purse for the key.

                    LORETTA
That's right . . . Bye-bye . . .

                    ANNIE (OS)
Bye-bye!

                    ANOTHER VOICE
                (higher, stilted chirp)
Bye-bye . . .

                    LORETTA
That's right, bye—
                (does a double-take)
Tracy?
                        (stares)
That *you,* Tracy?

Tracy's expression gives no clue. Loretta creeps low, as if Tracy might startle like a bird and fly away.

                    LORETTA
Bye-bye . . . Bye-bye, Tracy.

Eyes on the TV, Annie answers on autopilot. Loretta gently takes Tracy from Annie's lap, sits her down on the sofa and crouches in front of her.

                    LORETTA
C'mon Tracy . . . Bye-bye.
                    (a beat)
Say bye-bye. . . .

                    TRACY
Bye-bye . . .

Loretta pulls Tracy close and starts to cry.

LORETTA

Oh, Tracy . . . That's a good girl, such a good girl . . .

*Earl, Thomas and Zenia quietly appear in various doorways. Loretta holds
Tracy at arm's length.*

LORETTA

Can you say "Mama"?
(*coaxes*)
C'mon . . . Ma . . . Ma.

Tracy thinks hard, then:

TRACY

Bye-bye!

*Loretta laughs through tears as an excited Thomas joins her. Earl stands in the
doorway, beaming.*

INT. JUST CHICKEN—DAY

*Loretta expertly works the busy register. Earl wanders over, at a loss for
something to do.*

LORETTA

You know, I been thinkin' . . .

EARL
(*guarded*)
Uh-oh. What you been thinkin' this time?

LORETTA

About puttin' in a suggestion box.

EARL
(*rolls his eyes*)
You ready for a break yet?

LORETTA

You done asked me that five minutes ago. Why don't
you walk 'round and talk with the customers?
(off his puzzlement)
You know, askin' them if things are OK?
(off his doubt)
Go on. . . . Just give it a try.

*Earl awkwardly approaches two DINERS enjoying their meal. It takes them a
few moments to notice his forced smile.*

EARL

How's your lunch?

The diners exchange bemused looks.

DINER 1

Well . . . It's just fine.

DINER 2

Never had horseradish-cilantro-creamed chicken
before.

Carl enters, looking worried.

LORETTA

Hey, Carl. Same ol', same ol'?

CARL

Earl around?

*Carl motions for Earl to follow him outside, where they talk. Through the
window, Loretta can see that it can't be a pleasant conversation. Earl glumly
reenters.*

EARL

There goes the town. They shuttin' down the chicken
plant.

INT. JUST CHICKEN—LATE AFTERNOON

About a dozen TOWN LEADERS discuss their options. Loretta, Gina, and Isabelle pretend to clean while listening in.

> CITIZEN ONE
>
> How 'bout a picket line in front of the plant?

> CITIZEN TWO
>
> Now, what's *that* s'posed to do?

> CITIZEN ONE
>
> It worked for Martin in sixty-four, didn't it?
> *(looks for support)*
> What you think, Earl?

Lost in thought, Earl just shakes his head.

EXT. EARL'S CHURCH—LATE AFTERNOON

Closed and peaceful during midweek.

The stillness is interrupted by the approach of Earl's car. It turns into the empty gravel parking area.

INT./EXT. EARL'S PARKED CAR—LATE AFTERNOON

Earl and Loretta are dressed as in the previous restaurant scenes. Earl turns off the engine and pensively gazes towards the cemetery.

> EARL
>
> "Consolidation," just to save a few dollars. Closin' the
> plant is gonna take food off the tables of two hundred
> families.

Loretta uneasily observes Earl silently step from the car and walk towards the cemetery without looking back.

A few beats of uncertainty, then she exits the car to follow.

EXT. CHURCH CEMETERY — LATE AFTERNOON

Loretta approaches Earl, who's seated on the huge tree stump, pondering the many headstones and absorbing the stillness.

>   LORETTA
> You OK . . . ?

>   EARL
> A hundred fifty years of family history, and it all ends
> right here. . . .
>   *(a few beats)*
> You know, for a while, right after the Civil War,
> Nathan was buried here, too.

Loretta's eyes flicker across the many headstones. Earl pats the flat top of the stump beside him.

>   EARL
> No, right here, at the base of his favorite tree.

>   LORETTA
> Why?

>   EARL
> During the last days of the Civil War, there were no
> real laws . . .

We FLASHBACK. . . .

EXT. SINCLAIR HOUSE — NIGHT — 1865

A small Union camp of ragged tents and campfires. DRUNKEN REVELERS — black and white — spill out the front door of the neglected house onto the porch.

> EARL (VO)
> Just a bunch of wild northern soldiers and freed slaves
> . . . all running 'round, tryin' to get their hands on
> anything they could find. Jesse took Nathan right off
> the fireplace mantel of our house. . . .

EXT. CEMETERY TREE STUMP — PRESENT

> LORETTA
> (intrigued smile)
> Jesse stole it?

> EARL
> No, he *protected* it. Buried Nathan deep, right here, next
> to this tree. Then he took off out of town till things
> settled down. He dug Nathan back up and kept him
> safe in his sharecropper's shack, hidden away under the
> bed.

> LORETTA
> Mama keeps Nathan hidden away, too. Last few years,
> she's been keeping him locked away at the church. . . .

> EARL
> A old Sinclair family tradition. Doing whatever it takes
> to protect Nathan from anyone who might bring harm
> to him.

Loretta's eyes shift to register a twinge of guilt.

EARL (VO)

Anyway, the only time Jesse brought Nathan out was
to talk to him.

LORETTA

To talk to him?

INT. SHARECROPPER'S SHACK — 1890

*A YOUNG WOMAN cooks in the fireplace. Two small CHILDREN come
scampering in the front door, and she shoos them back outside, then stares across
the room, shaking her head.*

EARL (VO)

His wife and kids thought he was a little crazy. . . .

A YOUNG MAN beside the bed holds and speaks to the candelabra.

EARL (VO)

But any time Jesse had a problem, he'd just pull
Nathan right out from under the bed, sit down and talk
it over with him. Used to say that talkin' things out with
Nathan gave him hope, made him remember that
tomorrow's another day.

EXT. CEMETERY TREE STUMP — PRESENT

EARL

Ever since things started goin' wrong with Annie . . . all
I could think 'bout was Will and Nathan. . . . Gettin'
'em both back here to the Delta . . . I sure do wish I
had Nathan to talk things over with now. . . .

LORETTA

There's got to be *somethin'* we can do.

EARL

No. I think we've gone about as far as we were meant
to go. I'm seventy years old, Loretta. . . . Nathan's long
gone to Chicago, Will's in Atlanta, and now the town's
about to go, too.

(standing, weary)

Maybe it's time for me and Annie to live things out as
best we can.

Earl walks towards the car. Loretta looks at the headstones for some sign of the
future, then calls after him:

LORETTA

How about expandin' the restaurant? Wouldn't that
make some more jobs for people?

Earl shakes his head at her naiveté.

INT. LIVING ROOM — DAY

Annie and Tracy watch that same episode of "I Love Lucy." Thomas numbly
stares out the window and perfectly lip-syncs the dialogue. His eyes widen.

WHAT HE SEES: Two deer, one of them quite young, cautiously emerge from
the trees.

Thomas races toward the stairs.

EXT. FRONT PORCH — DAY

Thomas races out with his camera and moves quickly to the end of the porch. He
crouches there, aims his camera, and waits, finger on the button.

WHAT HE SEES: Through the lens, the corner of the house right in front of
us. Our view trembles a bit.

Thomas holds his breath and steadies his hands.

BACK THROUGH THE LENS: Then the deer are looking right at us, and we snap the picture.

The deer bound away. Thomas sits and waits for the picture to develop. Far behind him, Annie shuffles out to the steps. As she labors down, Thomas stares at his Polaroid:

> THOMAS
>
> C'mon . . . C'mon . . .

Tracy flies out the door squealing, getting Thomas's attention just in time to see her grab Annie around the legs, and they tumble down. Thomas drops camera and picture.

Tracy shakes herself off, but Annie lies still, moaning. When Thomas looks in her open eyes, he sees nothing.

> THOMAS
>
> Zenia! . . . ZENIA!!

INT. JUST CHICKEN—DAY

Loretta looks bemusedly at Carl, who awkwardly pays his bill.

> CARL
> *(trace of shyness)*
> You know, we really gonna miss seein' you 'round the place.

> LORETTA
> *(small realization)*
> That's real sweet, Carl. But we'll be back to visit.

> EARL
> *(dark mutter)*
> Better make that visit real soon.

Earl answers the ringing telephone.

                              EARL
Just Chicken.
                          (eyes widen)
Whoa, slow down, Zenia. . . .

Loretta, working the register, catches the tone of his voice.

                              EARL
Uh-huh.
                         (looks at Loretta)
Now you listen to me. . . . Don't you try movin' her till
they get there, you understand?! . . . I'm on my way!

He hangs up the phone and heads for the door.

                              EARL
C'mon. Annie's taken a bad fall.

EXT. HOSPITAL — DAY

Establishing shot of a small, brick county hospital.

INT. WAITING ROOM — DAY

*Earl and Loretta wait quietly. When DR. RAINEY enters, carrying an X-ray,
they stand.*

                          DR. RAINEY
Mr. Sinclair, your wife's left hip is broken. It's a serious
situation — we need to reset the hip, but she's still in
shock, making the procedure somewhat risky.

                              EARL
What does that mean?

                          DR. RAINEY
It means we would normally postpone the procedure
until the patient stabilizes, but it's difficult to tell when
that happens with Alzheimer's patients.

EARL

What happens if we wait anyway?

DR. RAINEY

The longer we wait, the more likely some unexpected
movement will further damage the hip.
(Earl absorbs this)
And the sooner we reset the hip, the more likely that
she'll be able to walk again.
(a beat)
If she's still . . . able to learn how to walk at that time.
(another beat)
I think we should go ahead with it.

Earl stares at the consent forms, then reaches for the pen.

LATER, SAME LOCATION

Earl stares up at the ceiling as, in the background, Loretta hangs up the corridor
payphone and reenters.

EARL

How's Thomas holdin' up?

Loretta indicates "so-so," and sits down.

LORETTA

I hope I never have to face makin' a decision like that.

EARL

Wasn't all that hard. Woulda been, if operatin' meant
the difference between life and death.
(ponders)
That's the one I've always been afraid of. Havin' to
decide if it's right to keep her alive, when I know her
mind is gone.

SAME LOCATION — EVENING

They stand when Dr. Rainey again approaches.

DR. RAINEY

From an immediate physical perspective, it went very well.

LORETTA

Oh, thank God . . .

DR. RAINEY

It was a very clean break, so all we basically had to do was reset the hip.

Earl grips the doctor's hand.

EARL

Thank you, Dr. Rainey . . . so much . . .

DR. RAINEY

It'll take a few hours of observation to see what happens when the anesthesia wears off.
                    (turning away)
We'll let you know, the minute there's a change.

Earl follows him out the door.

EARL

I gotta go call Will.

SAME LOCATION — NIGHT

Earl has started to doze off. He opens his eyes to find Loretta thoughtfully observing him.

EARL

What you thinkin' about?

LORETTA

You. You and Aunt Annie. The way you are about her.
                    (shakes her head)
If it were the other way around — she lookin' after you — I guess I'd understand it better. I mean . . . most all women stand by their men. Not too many men stand by their women.

EARL
(*stares off*)
When we were little kids, we used to work the same
field. She was this . . . skinny, *skinny* little thing. . . .
(*pauses*)
Draggin' that big sack of cotton behind her . . . Always
gettin' in the way or fallin' way behind. . . .
(*soft smile*)
Now I came from a big family, and I never had much
food to bring along for lunch. And then one day . . .
(*tears starting*)
One day, she shared her food with me. . . .
(*breaks down*)
And I saw she wasn't so skinny anymore. . . .

Loretta goes to his side, draws him close to cradle his head.

LORETTA
It's OK, go on . . . Let somebody take care of you for a
change.

SAME LOCATION — DAWN

Earl and Loretta are awakened in their chairs by Will's arrival. Earl stands and hugs his son.

WILL
I know you said I shouldn't come, but . . .
(*voice catching*)
But she's my mother. . . .

Loretta slips out to give them some privacy.

INT. HOSPITAL CORRIDOR — MORNING

Loretta comes out of the restroom to see Earl and Will outside of Annie's recovery room, quietly disagreeing about something.

Earl looks up and sees her, and they walk over to her. Loretta looks at Earl quizzically, and he shakes his head.

> EARL
>
> They gonna try a different medication.
> Listen, Will's gonna take you home for a while.
> *(cuts off her protest)*
> Now don't fight me on it. Just long 'nough for you to
> get some real sleep.

Will and Loretta exchange unenthusiastic looks.

EXT. HOUSE — DAY

Thomas waits in a porch rocker, glumly staring at a Polaroid picture. He stands as Will's rental car pulls in. When Loretta reaches him, she puts her arms around him to comfort him.

> THOMAS
>
> I'm sorry, Mama. . . .

> LORETTA
>
> I know you are, baby, and so does Uncle Earl.
> *(he starts to cry)*
> She's gonna be OK. . . . She's gonna be just fine. . . .

Will picks up the Polaroid left in the rocker.

> WILL
>
> Where'd this come from?

Will shows it to Loretta, who takes a breath.

WHAT SHE SEES: *Two beautiful, inquisitive deer, as though photographed for* National Geographic.

                    LORETTA
This is . . . just . . . amazin'. *Amazin'!*
                    (eyes Thomas's despair)
You know what? I think this would make a fine "get
well" present for Aunt Annie.

                    THOMAS
You really think so?

                    LORETTA
Yes, I really do.

                    WILL
                    (awkwardly)
You know, Mama used to come out early in the
morning and sit on the porch and wait for the deer. I
think she'd really like seeing them again.

Thomas brightens. Loretta eyes Will with new respect.

                    LORETTA
You hungry?

INT. KITCHEN — DAY

*Loretta puts finishing touches on a plate of sausages and sides. Will enters in a
fresh change of clothing.*

                    LORETTA
All we got 'round this place is chicken stuff. . . .

As Loretta puts some dirty dishes in the sink, Will digs in.

                    WILL
This is about the only thing I miss about Marianna.

                    LORETTA
                    (eyes his gusto)
You pullin' my leg. Like you can't find a decent sausage
in Atlanta?

                    • 129 •

WILL

Pork sausage, but not chicken sausage. Eat enough pork sausage, they all start to taste the same. Little-known fact: the older you get, the more your taste buds have trouble telling different flavors. We're all getting older. That's why spicy foods are getting pretty trendy.

LORETTA
(*idea sparked*)

Trendy . . . ?

WILL

Yeah. And with chicken replacing red meat, it's just a matter of time before people get tired of all the watered-down chicken out there.

LORETTA
(*mind whirling*)

So maybe they should be eating more spicy kinds of chicken . . . ?

WILL

Really. Somebody oughtta tell the rest of the world about my dad's twenty-eight different flavors of spicy chicken sausages.

Loretta's eyes widen, and she sits down across from him.

LORETTA

Hey, Will? . . . What you know 'bout . . . "entre-preneural sausage" . . . ?

We BEGIN A MONTAGE, where Loretta's idea unfolds:

INT. KITCHEN — LATE AFTERNOON

Will and Loretta are still talking at the kitchen table, with the meal cleared away and the light fading.

INT. CHICKEN PLANT — DAY

Carl shows Will and Loretta some dated equipment. Curious and concerned WORKERS strain to eavesdrop.

INT. HOSPITAL WAITING ROOM — EVENING

Will and Loretta are seated across from Earl. He listens skeptically as they excitedly interrupt each other.

INT. CHICKEN PLANT OFFICE — DAY

A large window overlooks the processing area below. Will and Loretta are talking to two intrigued PLANT MANAGERS.

INT. JUST CHICKEN — EVENING

Our MONTAGE CONCLUDES with another meeting of town leaders. It's a full house, and everyone attentively listens to Will.

> WILL
>
> People today are eating *twice* as much chicken as they did just ten years ago . . .
> > *(excited murmurs)*
>
> And *that* factory . . .
> > *(points out the window)*
>
> Is *just* as good for processing chicken into ready-to-heat-n-eat as it is for just cutting it up!
> > *(off scattered applause, to himself)*
>
> I hope.

Off Will's "gospel," Loretta and Earl exchange bemused looks.

> WILL
>
> People, look at the *opportunity* all around you! "Just Chicken" recipe books! A nationwide chain of "Just Chicken" restaurants! I swear, someday "Just Chicken" could be bigger than King Cotton *ever* was!

As the crowd stands to applaud, Will motions and Earl prods for Loretta to join him. As she walks up, Will steps aside. The applause dies and people smile and wait. More to herself:

LORETTA

Ain't nobody gonna do it for us. . . .

CITIZEN THREE (OS)

No, they're not. . . .

LORETTA
(confidence grows)

Can we do it for ourselves?

CITIZEN THREE (OS)

Yes, we can. . . .

LORETTA
(thought occurring)

Can we? . . . *Can* we do it?
(affirmative responses)

Yes, we can! We can *do* it!
(prompting chant)

We can *do* it! . . . We can *do* it!
(claps, encourages)

We *can* do it! . . . We *can* do it!
(continues over)

The chanting builds, hands clap and feet stomp. Loretta notices Will politely clapping but edging away, and she goes to him to draw him back. He good-naturedly resists, until she gives him a mock "no-nonsense" look:

LORETTA
(eye contact, personal chant)

We can do it. . . . *We* can do it. . . .

WILL
(still resisting)

Uh-*uhhhhh* . . . *You* can do it. . . . *You* can do it . . .

They're cracking up, but Will allows Loretta to pull him back to center stage, where they "up" the volume, grinning side by side, in perfect rhythm.

Chanting and clapping in the back, Earl's own beaming, ear-to-ear grin reflects his pride. The mural on the wall behind him: AND THE CHICKEN SHALL INHERIT THE EARTH.

EXT. HOSPITAL PARKING LOT—DAY

Earl and Loretta walk Will to his rental car.

> WILL
>
> Finding the right food company won't be easy, so don't get your hopes too high. I'll do what I can from Atlanta, and in the meantime, find you a good attorney in Jackson.

> EARL
>
> It still sounds like you'll be comin' around here more often.

Will smiles, opens the car door and reaches in to start the engine and air conditioner.

> WILL
>
> Yeah, I guess it does.
> *(turns to Loretta)*
> You know, you really should come spend some time with us in Atlanta, get to know that branch of the family better.
> *(smiles)*
> Like you said, we've got a big, fancy house with plenty of space . . .

> LORETTA
> *(smiles back)*
> I'd like that. And if you and Monica ever make it to Chicago, you can stay with us. We'll chase out the rats, toss an extra mattress on the floor. . . .

Will gets into his car, and it eases from its space.

Earl thoughtfully observes the car turn from the lot.

EARL

Well . . . There he goes. . . .

LORETTA

You gonna be OK with that?

EARL
(accepting smile)

Yeah . . .

Earl and Loretta stroll back towards the hospital entrance.

EARL

You know, I really could use you here. I'm gettin' too
old to be takin' on new projects.

LORETTA

I did think 'bout it. But there's Rosa Lynn . . .
(shakes her head)
She ain't goin' nowhere. And since I'll be workin',
maybe I can find some kinda special school to help
Tracy. Besides, there's some leftover business waiting
up there I gotta take care of. It's just time to get on with
things. . . .

A few steps in silence, then:

EARL

What if I handed the restaurant over to you? That'd
give you something strong to start out with. . . . Give
me more time to spend with Annie.

LORETTA
(at a loss)

Well. I don't know what to say.
(ponders)
Certainly is something to think about. . . .

INT. HOSPITAL — DAY

As they enter, Dr. Rainey gets their attention.

> DR. RAINEY
>
> Mr. Sinclair . . .
> *(off their wariness)*
> It's good news.
> *(reaches them)*
> Annie's responding to the new medication, something is
> going on inside her mind. She's even making little
> sounds of some kind.

> EARL
>
> What kindsa sounds?

> DR. RAINEY
>
> Little moans mainly, but they're not moans of pain. It's
> as if she's trying to say something. I can't be sure, but
> it sounds a little bit like "Mama." Is her mother by any
> chance still alive?

Earl and Loretta lock eyes.

INT. ANNIE'S HOSPITAL ROOM — DAY

*They move past the medical apparatus to Annie's side. Her eyes are closed as
Loretta gingerly takes her hand.*

> LORETTA
>
> Annie? It's me, Annie, your mama.
> *(long moment)*
> C'mon, Annie. . . . Tell Mama you're OK. . . .

Her eyes closed, Annie's curls her fingers a bit around Loretta's:

> ANNIE
>
> Maaa . . .

Loretta cries as she folds Annie's hand between her own.

LORETTA

That's right . . . Mama's here with you, baby. . . . I'm gonna stay right here. . . .

GO TO BLACK.

EXT. EARL'S FRONT YARD — DAY

Thomas is gently pushing a happily squealing Tracy in the swing. It is highly evocative of the happily squealing, swinging child we saw earlier in the Chicago park.

EXT. FRONT PORCH — DAY

Earl and Loretta exit the house, Earl jangling his key ring, and Loretta carrying a filled travel bag over her shoulder. As they step down from the porch, Zenia comes out of the house, carrying a package.

ZENIA

Here, you forgot your lunch. . . .

LORETTA
(taking it)

Oh, thanks. . . .

ZENIA

Just one more thing —

LORETTA
(eyes roll)
— I know, I know, eat only the food you packed for me.

ZENIA
(eyebrows rise)

I'm not your mother, eat any ol' thing you want. It's just this . . .
(hugs her)

Good luck.

LORETTA
(returning the hug)
Thanks . . .

Earl has reached the car and opened his door.

EARL
Come on, now, you gonna miss the bus. . . .

LORETTA
Come here Tracy, come give your mama a "bye-bye"
kiss. . . .

Tracy tumbles off the swing and races over, Thomas following.

TRACY
Bye-bye! Bye-bye! Bye-bye!

Loretta picks her up.

LORETTA
Bye-bye . . . Bye-bye, Tracy . . . Mama's gonna be home
real soon. . . . C'mon, give Mama a kiss. . . .

*Tracy dutifully does so, then immediately squirms to be put down. Once down,
she keeps hold of Loretta's hand.*

*Thomas approaches, and Loretta draws him to her side as they walk towards her
car door.*

LORETTA
Well, what you think?

THOMAS
(simple confidence)
I think you and Gramma Rosa be home real soon.

*Loretta smiles at him, caresses his head, passes Tracy's hand to his, and gets in
the car.*

INT. EARL'S CAR—DAY

As the car eases out of the drive and begins to gather speed along the country road, Loretta turns to look back.

WHAT SHE SEES: Standing in the road, framed by the canopy of willows: Zenia, Thomas and Tracy, all waving. Then, Tracy squirms loose and runs after the car, Thomas chasing.

Loretta gives one last wave, then turns back around to face the road ahead.

INT. ROSA LYNN'S APARTMENT—DAY

Loretta and Rosa Lynn are at the table. Rosa Lynn laughs and polishes Nathan with gusto.

> LORETTA
> *(gasping)*
> I swear, he was screamin' like a woman, over an itty-bitty, dead garden snake. . . .
> *(holds up index fingers)*
> No bigger'n a pencil, or a . . . a . . .
> *(space between fingers narrows)*

They lose it. Finally, Rosa Lynn catches her breath.

> ROSA LYNN
> Oh, Lord . . . I am gonna miss that boy.

> LORETTA
> *(turning serious)*
> I don't know why you won't come down and stay with us.

> ROSA LYNN
> Hmph! It's not *me* Earl wants down there, it's *you.* Only reason he wants me around's so he can get his hands on Nathan.

LORETTA

I guess he thinks if Nathan were down there, things
might start gettin' better again.

ROSA LYNN

He tell you to say that?

LORETTA

Not exactly, but I can just tell.

ROSA LYNN

Well, maybe Nathan needed to stay up here to look
after us after your father died. Earl ever stop to think
about that?
(leans towards her)
And who do you think Nathan's gonna be passed along
to, if he goes back down to the Delta? You thought
about *that*?

LORETTA

(holds up her hands in mock protection)
OK, OK. . . .

Rosa Lynn refocuses on her polishing task.

LORETTA

How come you never told me the whole story of
Nathan?

ROSA LYNN

When your father died, you were too young to really
understand it. Later on, I wasn't sure the time was ever
right for you to really *appreciate* it. I thought it was best
to just keep him put safely away till things got better.
(beat)
So Earl told you all about Nathan?

LORETTA
(nods)
How Jesse took it from the same people who kept him
as a slave. No wonder it meant so much to him.

ROSA LYNN
(trace of a smile)
But did Earl tell you about what happened to Jesse
when he was a little boy?
(off Loretta's blank look)
Jesse was just a little boy, when the white Sinclairs first
came over from Alabama. . . .

As she continues, we FLASHBACK. . . .

EXT. CROSSROADS COMMUNITY — 1854

Raw beginnings still being carved from swampy wilderness.

ROSA LYNN (VO)
They didn't come over with much, just their animals
and slaves.

An open-air barn, where a slave auction is in progress.

ROSA LYNN (VO)
And to get the land and things they needed, they had to
sell off a few of their slaves.

One SLAVE steps down from the block and another steps up. This SLAVE MAN
is in total anguish.

ROSA LYNN (vo)
Jesse was only six years old when he lost his father that
way, sold away right before his very eyes.

A distraught SLAVE WOMAN watches from a distance, being held back by
another, while a very young JESSE clutches her skirt.

ROSA LYNN (VO)

His mother never got over it, and Jesse never, ever, *ever* forgot it.

As young Jesse's eyes register fear and confusion . . .

INT. ROSA LYNN'S KITCHEN — PRESENT

Loretta's own are misty and staring at the candelabra.

LORETTA

So taking Nathan was Jesse's way of gettin' back at them. . . .

ROSA LYNN

In a way. He took the candelabra and set off to find his father. But he never did find him, not even a clue. After a while, he decided it was time to get on with things. So he went on back home and started a new family. And all his life, he did everything he could to keep his family together.
(*beat*)
And, Lord knows, sometimes that isn't easy. . . .

Loretta looks in her mother's eyes, directly and sincerely.

LORETTA

I can appreciate that.

Her now glistening eyes widen in realization:

LORETTA

Was Jesse's father named Nathan?

Rosa Lynn looks at her, gently smiles, and we FLASHBACK. . . .

EXT. SLAVE AUCTION — 1856

Again to young Jesse's expression of fear and confusion off the sounds of his mother's wails and the sight of his father being sold away. As his father turns to be led away, young Jesse's eyes lock with his, as though exchanging a final, silent communication.

> ROSA LYNN (VO)
> Yes, his name was Nathan . . .

Now we see what Jesse's Father was exchanged for: the silver candelabra.

> ROSA LYNN
> And he was traded away for a silver candelabra. . . .

His father gone, Young Jesse's eyes now close intently on the candelabra, as though to burn it into his memory. . . .

INT. ROSA LYNN'S KITCHEN — PRESENT

On Loretta's own crying eyes, until they eventually move from Nathan to Rosa Lynn.

> LORETTA
> Won't you at least *think* about it? That big ol' house got lotsa room. . . .

Rosa Lynn walks over to place Nathan on the TV-less stand.

> LORETTA
> What if you just come back down with me for a little visit?

Rosa Lynn admires the candelabra a few beats.

> ROSA LYNN
> Well . . . That might work out . . .
> (cuts off Loretta's glee)
> But you tell that Earl I don't want any of his foolishness, you hear me?!

EXT. MISSISSIPPI COUNTRY ROAD—DAY

Earl's car slowly meanders along.

EXT./INT. EARL'S CAR—DAY

Rosa Lynn stares out her window. Earl focuses on the road. Loretta's own eyes dart back and forth between the two.

EXT. EARL'S HOUSE—DAY

Earl unlocks the trunk for Loretta. While she pulls out luggage, he walks over to Rosa Lynn, who stares at the house.

EARL
Look about the same?
> *(she doesn't respond)*

We've made a lot of changes inside.

ROSA LYNN
I've never even been inside the big house before.

A school bus stops in the road to drop off Thomas. He runs, lugging his bulging knapsack.

THOMAS

Hey, Gramma Rosa . . .

ROSA LYNN
(they hug)
Well, aren't you a sight for these old eyes.
(admiring appraisal)
Where'd you get them fancy sneakers?

THOMAS

Mama got 'em for me.

Thomas brightens at the sight of Loretta holding Rosa Lynn's bulging canvas shopping bag.

THOMAS

You bring me a present, Mama?

LORETTA
(mock shock)
Is that all the welcome I get? Gimme, gimme, gimme?
(he grins)
You just slow down a minute. Tell me what school's like down here.

THOMAS
(ponders)
Different. They don't yell at you or search you or nothin'. It sure is hard, though.

Thomas takes the shopping bag to carry.

LORETTA

You take that on up to the house.
(calls after him)
And don't you touch nothin' till I get there, you hear me?!

Rosa Lynn's expression shows her private thrill of the New Loretta's words and tone.

> LORETTA
>
> So Will's been hangin' out with Annie at the hospital
> . . . How them two gettin' along?

> EARL
>
> *Amazingly* well. You should see them together . . . On
> Saturday, she asked if she could see his dress in a size
> ten, and you know what he did?

> LORETTA
>
> What?

> EARL
>
> He went out of the room and took off his suit jacket,
> and came back in and put it over her just like a little
> blanket. Now she won't let anybody else touch it!

Off Rosa Lynn's expression, they both grin.

INT. ENTRY HALL — DAY

Earl holds the door open for Rosa Lynn to enter. She gazes in wonder, trying to look nonchalant.

INT. LIVING ROOM — DAY

They enter to find Thomas waiting with the big shopping bag. Rosa Lynn looks around.

> ROSA LYNN
>
> Where's Tracy?

A sudden, delighted shriek, accompanied by a crash. Tracy bursts in from the kitchen and runs over to Rosa Lynn.

TRACY

Bye-bye! Bye-bye! Bye-bye! . . .

ROSA LYNN
(reaches down)
Well, aren't you Little Miss Amazin'?

Zenia enters, holding a broken plate. Loretta grins.

LORETTA

Hey, Zenia.

ZENIA

I'm *so* glad you're back.

LORETTA

I bet you are.

THOMAS
(prompting)
Mama . . .

LORETTA

Hold your horses, I brought back somethin' for
everyone.

She hands out gift-wrapped packages to everyone, even Tracy.

*Zenia smiles her appreciation before disappearing into the kitchen to privately
open her bottle-sized gift box.*

While Thomas unwraps his, Rosa Lynn helps Tracy.

ROSA LYNN

Let's see what you got, Tracy.

*It's a big, stuffed giraffe. Amidst "oohs" and "aahs," Tracy stares as Loretta
pulls the giraffe's string.*

LORETTA

Looky here, Tracy . . . This one really talks at you!

GIRAFFE
(dumb, mechanical voice)
My name is Jeffrey. . . . Will you be my friend?

Tracy shrieks in panic and punches it.

TRACY

Nooo!

LORETTA
(delighted)

Well, listen to you!

ROSA LYNN
You better get used to hearin' that one.

Tracy goes over to hug her mangled, loyal tiger.

THOMAS

Yo, looka this!

He admires a basic Kodak Instamatic, still in its box.

THOMAS
Man, it's dope-fresh new!

LORETTA
(pleased)
Ain't never been used by nobody.

Thomas holds it up to show Earl, and his eyes widen.

WHAT HE SEES: Earl tries to contain his emotions as he cradles the gleaming,
long lost Nathan.

Earl looks up at Rosa Lynn, who impassively holds his gaze until they conclude their silent communication. Then Earl slowly extends Nathan toward Loretta.

EARL
Here, Loretta . . . I guess he rightfully belongs to you.

Off Rosa Lynn's encouraging smile, Loretta awkwardly accepts the candelabra and stands there. A smile breaking, she walks over to the mantel and places Nathan to fill the empty space.

Thomas breaks the silence.

THOMAS
How come you call it Nathan, anyway?

Loretta waits first for Earl, then Rosa Lynn, but they just wait for her. She motions Thomas to join her on the sofa.

LORETTA

I'm gonna tell you a story about a family stayin'
together. You remember how Uncle Earl told you about
your . . .
(thinks back)
Great, great, great-grandfather Jesse . . . ?

*Off Thomas's nod and under her elders' approving smiles, she draws him a bit
closer and settles back. . . .*

LORETTA

Well, when Jesse was a little boy, just a few years
younger'n you . . .

FADE TO BLACK.

Showtime Presents

An AMEN RA FILMS and CHRIS/ROSE PRODUCTIONS Production

ALFRE WOODARD

Down in the Delta

AL FREEMAN, JR.

ESTHER ROLLE

MARY ALICE

LORETTA DEVINE

ANNE-MARIE JOHNSON

MPHO KOAHO

JUSTIN LORD

And
WESLEY SNIPES as "Will"

Casting by
REUBEN CANNON & ASSOCIATES

Music By
STANLEY CLARKE

Co-Producers
TERRI FARNSWORTH
MYRON GOBLE
ALFRE WOODARD

Edited By
NANCY RICHARDSON
Production Designer
LINDSEY HERMER-BELL

Director of Photography
WILLIAM WAGES, ASC

Produced By

RICK ROSENBERG & BOB CHRISTIANSEN

and

VICTOR McGAULEY & WESLEY SNIPES

and

REUBEN CANNON

Written By
MYRON GOBLE

Directed By
MAYA ANGELOU

C A S T

Loretta	ALFRE WOODARD
Earl	AL FREEMAN JR.
Rosa Lynn	MARY ALICE
Annie	ESTHER ROLLE
Zenia	LORETTA DEVINE
Will	WESLEY SNIPES

Thomas	MPHO KOAHO
Tracy	KULANI HASSEN
Monica	ANNE-MARIE JOHNSON
Dr. Rainey	JUSTIN LORD
Marco	RICHARD YEARWOOD
Volunteer	SANDRA CALDWELL
Tourist Woman	COLLEEN WILLIAMS
Tourist Man	RICHARD BLACKBURN
Manager	PHILIP AKIN
Drug Addict	MARY FALLICK
Pawnbroker	SANDI ROSS
Prim Woman	BARBARA BARNES HOPKINS
Prim Sister	MARIUM CARVELL
Gina	QUANCETIA HAMILTON
Isabelle	KIM ROBERTS
Reverend Floyd	DeFOY GLENN
Man in Congregation	JEFF JONES
Dozing Woman	MICHELYN EMELLE
Grinning Man	JOHNIE CHASE
Cassandra	ANDREA LEWIS
Carl	NIGEL SHAWN-WILLIAMS
Diner 1	BERNARD BROWNE
Diner 2	ALISON SEALY-SMITH
Citizen 1	EUGENE CLARKE
Citizen 2	CHRIS BENSON
Jesse's Wife	CAROL ANDERSON
Slave Man	NEVILLE EDWARDS
Slave Woman	YANNA McINTOSH
Collin	TROY SEIVWRIGHT-ADAMS
Justin	KEVIN DUHANEY
Jesse 1865 (17 years old)	JOEL GORDON
Jesse 1890 (42 years old)	PHIL JARRETT
Soloist in Church	CLINTON GREEN
Stunt Coordinator	WAYNE DOWNER
Annie Stunt Double	MELANIE NICHOLLS-KING
Production Manager	REGINA ROBB
First Assistant Director	MICHAEL ZENON
Second Assistant Director	ROCCO GISMONDI

Music Supervisor
TERRI FRICON

Costume Consultant
RUTH CARTER

Costume Designer
MAXYNE BAKER

Toronto Casting
ROSS CLYDESDALE, C.D.C.

Camera Operator	CHRISTOPHER TAMMARO
Focus Puller	CHRIS ALEXANDER
Second Assistant Camera	DIANA ALVAREZ
Camera Trainee	BRAD CROSBIE
Gaffer	FRANK TATA
Best Boy	MARK COWDEN
Electricians	SCOTT TREMBLAY
	ANTHONY RAMSEY
Generator Operator	JOHN SZTEJNMILER
Key Grip	DAVID "STRETCH" PAMPLIN
Best Boy	THOMAS CARE
Dolly Grip	STEPHEN LEMBERG
Grips	DIANNE HAGGARTY
	WILLIAM ENGEL

Assistant Editor	STACEY CLIPP
Production Coordinator	SHEENA GRAHAM
Assistant Production Coordinator	ANDREA FRANKS
In House Coordinator	VIRGINIA CAMPBELL
Assistant to Producers	GLENNIS BASTIEN
Script Supervisor	ANNA RANE
Production Accountant	KAREN de MONTBRUN
Assistant Production Accountant	KIM KILLAM
Comptroller	CATHERINE CURRIE
Post Production Accountant	B.E. SHARP
Third Assistant Director	ANTHONY TEDESCO
Trainee Assistant Director	CONROD CIANDRE
Office Coordinator	SHEELAGH STEWART
Production Assistants	ANTHONY GRANI
	GARETH BENNETT
Office Assistants	CHRISTINA MEYNELL
	CHANDRA-LI PAUL

Art Director	ROBERT SHER
Third Assistant Art Director	ANNA KISS
Set Decorator	MEGAN LESS
Lead Dresser	MICHAEL MULLINS
Set Buyer	ROB HEPBURN
Set Dressers	DAVID "ROCKY" ROCKBURN
	ANDY JOYCE

Property Master	PETER MISKIMMIN
Assistant Props Master	MARK HUNTER
Props Assistant	JENNIFER JACOBSEN
Key Makeup	LYNDA McCORMACK
Hairstylist	VERONICA CIANDRE
Hairstylist for Ms. Woodard	STERFON DEMINGS
Makeup Artist for Ms. Woodard	WYNONA PRICE
Wardrobe Supervisor	GERSHA PHILLIPS
Wardrobe Assistants	KOREANN CIANDRE
	STEVEN WRIGHT
Production Sound Mixer	TOM HIDDERLEY
Boom Operator	MOSHE SAADON
Post-Production Supervisor	TIM KING
Post-Production Coordinators	CYNTHIA NICOLELLA
	DAVID BAILEY
	CHAD TOMASOSKI
Post-Production Assistant	ROBERT RODRIGUEZ
Audio Post-Production	DIGITAL SOUND & PICTURE
Supervising Sound Editor	DEAN HOVEY
Re-Recording Mixers	PATRICK GIRAUDI
	JOE BARNETT
Sound Effects Editors	DORIAN CHEAH
	LISLE ENGLE
	ROLAND THAI
	MIKE MULLANE
ADR Supervisor	ROBERT JACKSON
Dialogue Editors	JASON GEORGE
	YURI REESE
	TOM JONES
	DAVID GRANT
	LOU CREVELING
	TROY ALLEN
	STEVE SCOVILLE
Foley Editors	TOM VOLCKMAN
	CRAIG JURKIEWICZ
	DAVE MARCUS
	TONY SURACI
Foley Mixer	MARY ERSTAD
Foley Artists	OSSAMA KHULUKI
	DIANE MARSHALL
	KEN DUFVA
ADR Mixer	ALAN FREEDMAN

Walla Group	STEVE & EDIE'S
Location Manager	RICHARD HUGHES
Assistant Location Manager	JOHN MENDES
Location Scout	CHRISTOPHER WELCH
Location Production Assistant	IAN SMITH
Special Effects Coordinator	TIM GOOD
Construction Coordinator	DWIGHT DOERKSEN
Head Carpenter	ROGER GELFAND
Assistant Head Carpenter	ED DOERKSEN
Carpenters	GEOFFREY EDGE
	ALAN MOY
Key Scenic Painter	MAURO IACOBELLI
Head Painter	STEPHEN PAISLEY
Scenic Painter	SEAN LIEBRECHT
Transport Supervisor	MARK VAN ALSTYNE
Transport Coordinator	JEROME McCANN
Transportation Captain	GRANT WILKINS
Drivers	DOUGLAS BARKLEY
	DENNIS BRESSAN
	GLEN CRESSWELL
	CHERYL DARBEY
	ALEX LAFRAMBOISE
	GERALD POWLENZUK
	STEVEN SACROB
	EVAN SIEGEL
	CARL SEVERIN
	STEVE WARREN
	MICHAEL WILKIN
Picture Vehicle Coordinator	ERWIN ROITHMEIER
Stills Photographer	BEN MARK HOLZBERG
Unit Publicist	ROB HARRIS
Caterer	BY DAVID'S CATERING
Craft Service	STARCRAFT
Acting Coach	ALISON SEALY-SMITH
L.A. Casting Associate	EDDIE DUNLOP
Extras Casting	ELEANORE LAVENDER
Music Consultant	LARRY GREENE
Music Editor	DEAN RICHARD MARINO
Music Clearance	GAY DiFUSCO
Stereo Consultants	J. LOUIS DURAN, JR.
	FRED RIVAS
Film Laboratory	DELUXE

Titles & Opticals   F-STOP, INC.
Negative Cutter   VIVKIM
Color Timer   MATVEY SHATZ
Color by   DELUXE
Lenses and Panaflex Cameras by   PANAVISION

Digital Post Production Provided by
BIG TIME PICTURE COMPANY

Production Services Provided
by
DUFFERIN GATE PRODUCTIONS INC.

Executive in Charge of Production
STEVE WAKEFIELD

SONGS

FULANI CHANT
Composed and Arranged by Aisha Kahill
Copyright 1985 Thunderhead Music, All Rights Reserved
Licensed by Frances J. Jones, Esq./Provision International, Inc.
Performed by Sweet Honey In The Rock
(p) 1992 EarthBeat! Records
Courtesy of EarthBeat! Records

PATCHWORK QUILT
Words and Music by Michelle Lanchester
Published by Mikkel Music
Performed by Sweet Honey In the Rock
(p) 1992 EarthBeat! Records
Courtesy of EarthBeat! Records

Copyright © 1998
This Motion Picture
Down In The Delta Productions, LP
This Screenplay
Down In The Delta Productions, LP

DOWN IN THE DELTA

a presentation of SHOWTIME NETWORKS INC.
A Viacom Company